MAGNETIC
FEMALE ENTREPRENEUR

The Art of Empowered Presence, Rising to New Levels of Impact and Influence, and Financial Success on Your Own Terms

MARY GRANT

Ink & Impact Press
WHERE VISIONS BECOME REALITY

In the world of entrepreneurs, there are those who lead and those who follow the crowd.

Those who lead are the trailblazers. When everyone else goes right, they go left.

They set the trends, rewrite the rules, and create success on their own terms.

They set their sights on a vision or mission and pursue it relentlessly.

They lean into creating meaningful impact, fearlessly stepping beyond their comfort zones to expand their reach and amplify their influence.

They harness their superpowers and unleash their secret sauce.

They are magnetic, attracting clients and opportunities like bees to a honey pot.

They transcend the ordinary... for them, there are no limits.

This book is for entrepreneurs, business owners and coaches who are ready to step into their next level or chapter, be magnetic and become unstoppable.

CONTENTS

UNLEASH YOUR
SECRET SAUCE

PART 1

YOUR SECRET SAUCE

In a world where attention is the new currency, everyone is competing for it. Experts are selling countless ways to build your business, each with their formula for success. But in the rush to follow these paths, we often overlook one of the most valuable assets we have – what makes us uniquely powerful.

Your journey, the challenges you've overcome, the strengths you've honed, and the values you hold dear are all part of your secret sauce. It's the combination of these elements – your innate superpowers, your brand personality, your beliefs, and your stories that sets you apart. Yet, too often, we step over this goldmine, hiding because we're afraid of being truly seen.

But what if you took the time to uncover the treasure that's uniquely yours? Imagine turning this hidden gold into a foundation so solid that it becomes the rock you stand on-a rock that elevates you above the noise, making you a beacon for those who need exactly what you offer.

In this section, we're going on a treasure hunt. We're mining for the gold within you so that you can build a brand that stands head and shoulders above the crowd. It's time to unlock your secret sauce and let your true power shine.

CHAPTER 1

TREASURES FROM YOUR PAST

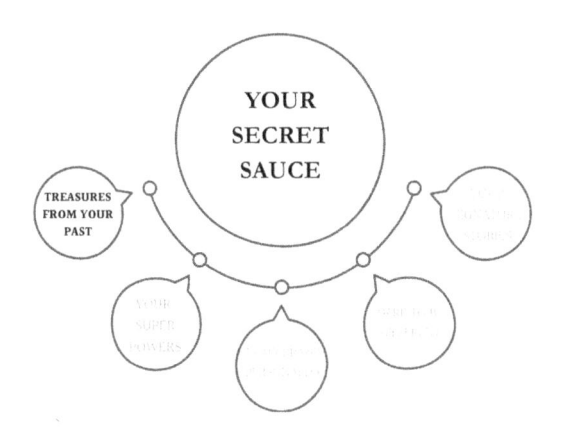

Lorraine is a very successful entrepreneur with a head for numbers that makes *my* head spin. She is the backbone of the property investment business she runs with her husband. Despite having a very full life with two teenage kids and a love for travel, Lorraine felt she still had more to do. She has a burning desire to create an impact in the lives of women, separate from the family business. Like many women with a track record of success, she is multi-talented with many interests. How could she focus on just one?

The problem with finding your own secret sauce is that sometimes you can be standing too close to your own story. You can't see the wood for the trees. So, we booked a personal brand session, one of my favourite things to do. These sessions are like treasure hunts ... where you always find treasure!

In our deep dive session, we went right back to her childhood. The signposts to her future career path were right there in how she spent her time as a child, but like so many of us, she was stepping right over them. She could lose herself for hours sorting and rearranging her father's garden shed and laying blocks into the outlines of houses on the grass.

Over the course of two hours, we followed the golden threads of her curiosity right through her life, picking up insights and aha moments along the way. By the time we got to a question I love to ask, "If you had a magic wand, what would you create right now?" Without missing a beat, Lorraine was able to tell me the name of her future mastermind, her podcast, and her book. Lorraine was shocked. "I think you just changed my life," she said.

When you pull out the golden threads of your past and see the journey they've woven, your future roadmap comes into clear focus, and the distractions naturally fall away, revealing what truly matters.

Overlooking your past

In all the personal brand sessions I've conducted, many people can list most of their transferable skills, but every single person has been stepping over the things that are unique to them that they take for granted. I include myself in this.

Recently, I found myself in front of my coach, expressing my desire to keep my fashion business and coaching business separate. I believed that the crossover was confusing for everyone, including me. By doing this, I was denying myself a treasure chest of experience and insights. These were the very things that could benefit the people I felt called to serve. This realisation was a big wake-up call for me. And let me tell you, convincing me was not easy!

Every experience, success, failure, mentor, influence, challenge, and even those seemingly insignificant moments are part of your unique story. These elements are what set you apart. These are the ingredients of your secret sauce. Everything you collect on life's journey is a goldmine of clues pointing towards a clear, authentic path forward. By acknowledging and embracing these aspects, you can craft a future that truly reflects who you are and what you stand for. When you fully embrace and utilise these strengths, you not only differentiate yourself from others but also find a heightened sense of alignment and authenticity in your work and life.

Rather than just powering through this book, please stop and do the work! You are leaving all the gold behind if you are just consuming content rather than harnessing your own personal insights. So, grab your journal, take the time to ponder your past and harvest the treasure chest of golden nuggets that make you who you are today.

9 ways to find the treasures from your past

Childhood joys

Think back to how you loved to spend your time as a child. What activities brought you the most joy and fulfilment? What activities captured your attention that made time fly by? These early interests can be powerful indicators of your innate talents, strengths and destiny. Think about how these interests have shown up along your life's journey.

School favourites

What subjects did you love in school? Which teachers or classes made a significant impact on you? Reflect on the topics and educators that inspired you. Go beneath the surface here and think about why that subject appealed to you. Did you excel in science because you loved problem-solving, or did history captivate you with its rich narratives? Or maybe it was geography because you were fascinated with eco-systems or far-flung places? These preferences can reveal patterns in your interests and strengths.

College choices

What did you study in college, and why? How did those choices reflect your passions and interests at the time? Consider the courses and activities you were drawn to during your college years. Whether you majored in a specific field or participated in extracurricular activities, these choices can provide insights into your enduring interests. Start to observe the golden nuggets of your past and the threads that connect them.

Influential people and events

Who are the key people and what are the key events that have shaped your journey and beliefs? Reflect on the mentors, family members, and friends who have influenced you. Consider the significant events that have impacted your life. These influences can help you understand your core values and how they align with your personal and professional goals. (At the end of this chapter, we will look at changing any stories that may have had a negative impact on you- because let's face it, we all have those monsters hiding under the bed!)

Skill-set

What skills have you gathered along the way? Consider how these skills are transferable to different areas of your life and work. Whether you've developed technical skills, leadership abilities, or creative talents, recognise the value they bring to your personal and professional life. Your diverse skill set is a crucial element of your secret sauce. Zoom out and observe the over-arching themes.

Your success reel

What are your standout successes? What led you there, what skills and innate talents do you step over because they come so naturally to you? Celebrate your achievements and think about what made them possible. Identify the qualities and actions that contributed to your success. Was it your perseverance, strategic thinking, or ability to lead others? These highlights can provide clues to your unique strengths and capabilities.

Following your natural trail of curiosity

Think back to the moments when your curiosity led you down unexpected paths. These natural trails of curiosity are significant indicators of your passions and potential strengths. They are the breadcrumbs that, when followed, reveal your innate interests and unique talents. Observe where in your past you made choices that brought you to places you never expected to go. I love observing these because it builds a trust in yourself to keep moving forward in the future, even if you don't have full clarity on your next steps.

Standout stories

Reflect on the standout stories of your past. What meaning do they hold for you? How did they shape who you are today? Think about the pivotal moments in your life that have defined you. These stories highlight your resilience, creativity, leadership style and a whole host of natural abilities and build a powerful story of who you authentically are and what makes you unique.

Lessons learned

Reflect on the lessons you've learned from both your successes and failures. Every experience, whether positive or negative, has shaped who you are today and provided valuable insights. What challenges have you overcome, and what did they teach you about your resilience and capabilities? Understanding these lessons is crucial for leveraging your past to inform your future decisions and actions and build an unshakeable trust in yourself that as you move forward, the path will be revealed.

Pro-tip: reframing past stories

Aside from obvious unjust and horrible things that may have happened in your past, there are so many stories that we hold onto that do not serve us. Sometimes get stuck in the stories we tell ourselves because we are not aware of how easily we can change their meaning.

You can change the meaning of any story, looking for the lessons learned or the new directions they took you in. Not only that but you can keep revisiting those stories, changing their meaning from the perspective of where you are now and in the future. The person who experienced that story initially does not exist today because you have grown and evolved since then. The person you will be in a year's time will be able to gather a whole new meaning from the same story.

Example: Old Story: "I failed at my first business because I wasn't good enough." Reframed Story: "My first business taught me invaluable lessons that set me up for success in my current venture."

By reframing past stories, you empower your present and create a positive narrative that supports your growth.

The lessons from your past serve as a reminder of how powerful you are but we all need that reminder sometimes so, whenever you find yourself second-guessing yourself, ask yourself this question:

"What past experiences am I overlooking that hold the clues to my future success?"

CHAPTER 2

YOUR SUPERPOWERS

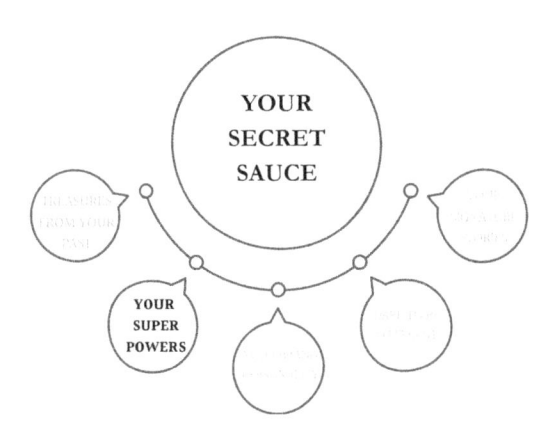

Before I stepped into the online business world, I had never heard of any of the personality tests that are part of normal everyday language in the online world. From Myers-Briggs to the Enneagram, Human Design, and Clifton Strengths, these assessments can reveal powerful insights about who you are that you may be stepping over.

You might have your own favourites. The most powerful for me was Clifton Strengths. Clifton gives you two different levels of reports, your top 5 strengths or all 34 in order.

Honestly, the top five were enough for me as my interest is in focusing on my top strengths and getting better and better at those. I spent an hour journaling on where each of the top five showed up in my business and my life. This was more revealing than knowing the strengths themselves. It helped me to see where using them has impacted my success. It's important to not only know your strengths but also to recognise how they manifest in your daily life and work. This awareness allows you to be intentional about playing to your strengths and delegate tasks that don't align with them.

I've also developed my own personality assessments: *The Style Archetypes* for my book *Unleash Your Inner Goddess* and *The Personal Brand Archetypes* for personal brand owners. These tools have provided even deeper layers of actionable understanding for my clients, helping them to uncover their unique strengths and use them to their advantage. We will dive into the Personal Brand Archetypes in the next chapter.

Levelling up: playing to strengths vs. being busy

One of the words I have deleted from my vocabulary is 'busy'. When people ask me, "Are you busy?" I cringe. For years, I wore 'busy' like a badge of honour, constantly juggling tasks and responsibilities. It wasn't until I restructured my business in 2020 that I stepped away from being busy and started focusing on what truly matters.

Wearing 'busy' as a badge of honour can keep you stuck in a cycle of constant activity without meaningful progress. It's a trap that can lead to burnout and dissatisfaction. Since simplifying my business and aligning it with my strengths, I've found that I can run it in just a few hours a week. This shift has freed up space for creativity, strategic thinking, and personal growth.

To truly level up, you need to focus on playing to your strengths rather than being busy. Knowing your top strengths allows you to get better and better at those and operate from your zone of genius. It's also beneficial to know the top strengths of everyone on your team. This creates a culture where everyone is operating from their strengths, leading to higher productivity, better collaboration, and more job satisfaction. It also allows you to delegate tasks more effectively, ensuring that the right people are doing the right jobs.

By embracing and leveraging your unique strengths, you move from merely being busy to becoming truly impactful in your work and life. It's about quality over quantity, depth over breadth, and excellence over mere activity.

Aligning strengths with core values to create purpose

Purpose isn't something you have to search for; it's something you already carry within you, ready to be activated through your actions and decisions. When you and your team operate from your zones of genius, aligned with your core values, you create a purpose-driven culture that thrives.

Reflect on where your strengths have guided you to make decisions that felt deeply authentic and true to who you are. These are often moments when you were in alignment with your core values – those guiding principles that define what's truly important to you. When your actions resonate with these values, they lead to greater fulfilment and success, because they are rooted in your true self.

By identifying these instances, you not only reinforce the connection between your strengths and your values but also ensure that your future decisions are intentional and aligned with who you truly are. This alignment is where real purpose is found — it's what drives meaningful impact both in your life and within your team.

The shadow side of your strengths

For every strength there is a shadow side or a flip side. For example, someone with a strong drive for achievement might struggle with burnout or perfectionism. A natural connector who values building relationships might find it hard to set boundaries or say no.

The shadow side isn't something to fear or suppress. Instead, it's an opportunity to deepen your self-awareness and harness your full potential. By acknowledging and understanding this side of yourself, you can turn what might have been a weakness into a source of power.

Talking about the shadow side openly can lead to more authentic relationships with your team, family, and even clients. It can be a powerful way to build trust and foster a culture of growth. Imagine a team where everyone is aware of their own and each other's shadow sides, supporting one another in turning these potential pitfalls into strengths.

Creating balance

The key to managing both your strengths and their shadow sides is balance. When you're aware of how these dynamics play out, you can take proactive steps to ensure that your strengths shine without being undermined by their shadow sides. For instance, if your strength is a strong drive for achievement, but its shadow side leads to burnout, you might implement boundaries to protect your well-being. If your strength lies in attention to detail, but this sometimes turns into perfectionism, practice embracing "good enough" and celebrating small wins.

By bringing both your strengths and their shadow sides into the light, you not only empower yourself but also set the stage for deeper connections and more authentic leadership. This balanced awareness can become a powerful tool in your journey, helping you navigate challenges with greater insight and resilience.

Reflect on the shadow sides

Take time to identify your top strengths and consider the shadow sides of those strengths. How have these played out in your life? What can you do to amplify your strengths while managing their potential downsides? Here's what I discovered when I journaled on mine:

	Strength	Shadow side
Achiever	I have a relentless drive to accomplish goals and tackle new challenges. My high energy and productivity help me stay focused on tasks and push through obstacles to reach success.	This relentless drive can lead to burnout, which has happened several times over 30 years running a business while raising three kids on my own. I also struggle with slowing down and celebrating achievements because I'm always onto the next goal.
Relator	I thrive in building deep, meaningful relationships with others. I value authenticity and genuine connections and love one-on-one interactions where I can share experiences and support others.	I find it challenging to build superficial connections, which can be necessary in certain professional settings. I also struggle with letting go of relationships that no longer serve me. I have seen this play out many times when I look back over the years!

Maximiser	I have a keen eye for excellence and am constantly seeking ways to enhance my own performance and the performance of others. I focus on strengths rather than weaknesses, striving for continuous improvement and growth.	My pursuit of excellence can sometimes lead to perfectionism (I'm a recovering perfectionist).
Futuristic	I have a forward-thinking mindset and am drawn to envisioning and planning for the future. I enjoy exploring possibilities and am adept at setting ambitious goals and charting a course to achieve them.	Sometimes, my focus on the future can make me appear overly optimistic, potentially underestimating the challenges that may arise along the way.

Strategic	I have a knack for seeing the big picture and identifying the most effective pathways to success. I love simplifying complex situations, weighing options, and making well-informed decisions that drive progress toward objectives.	My strategic thinking can sometimes lead to prioritising long-term goals over immediate needs, which might make me less interested in getting bogged down in minor details.

Get everyone on your team to do this and share it so everybody knows what everyone else's strengths are. This tool is a reminder of what makes you unique and how you can leverage your strengths to stand out and make an impact.

Whenever you find yourself questioning your direction or feeling overwhelmed, this question will serve as a guiding light, helping you stay aligned with your strengths and ensuring that you focus your energy where it will have the most significant impact.

"Am I operating from my zone of genius?"

CHAPTER 3

YOUR PERSONAL BRAND ARCHETYPE

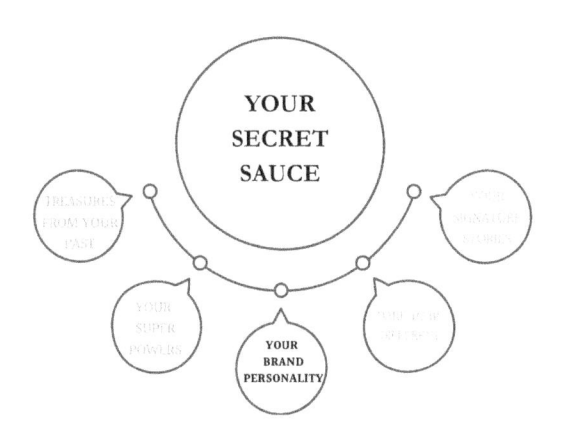

The first personality assessment I developed for my clients was when I was writing my first book, *Empowered by Style*, in 2019. (I have since rewritten this book, now entitled *Unleash Your Inner Goddess*.) The quiz to help my clients identify their style archetype has been running since 2018 and has helped hundreds of women to curate their closets, so they step out of their bedroom every morning ready to take on the world.

The *personal style archetypes* have been so popular that I thought it would be fun to create something similar for personal branding. While the style archetypes were based on the Myers-Briggs personality types, the *personal brand archetypes* take things to a new level. They build on the foundation of the *style archetypes*, enriched by insights gathered over the past five years and observations of women from all walks of life during my 30 years in the fashion industry. My goal in creating the *personal brand archetypes* is to offer another layer of insight that empowers entrepreneurs to step into their next level using their unique secret sauce. Each archetype represents a brand personality. By identifying your brand personality, you can infuse it into everything you do, from how you show up to how you connect with your ideal customers. Your brand personality adds a layer of authenticity and uniqueness that sets you apart from the competition.

There are nine brand personalities or archetypes. Their insights can be very revealing – I have learned a lot from my clients just by seeing their results in the assessment which you can take at **personalbrandarchetype.com** While the software can only tell you your top result, feel free to reach out to me for a full screenshot of your results. The true magic lies in the combination of your top three archetypes.

Remember, you're the one answering the questions. If your top result isn't what you expected, look at the next two and reflect on how they show up in your business interactions. I've included some possible shadow sides but don't take these are gospel. They are there to challenge your thinking! Remember, the power is in the insights – you can tip the scales towards whichever archetype you want to be more prominent!

THE INNOVATOR

The Innovator thrives on breaking new ground and introducing revolutionary ideas. They excel in environments that demand creativity and foresight, always ready to disrupt the status quo with the next big thing.

Self-discovery

As an Innovator, you are a visionary who transforms ideas into reality. Your unique ability to foresee possibilities and shape the future defines your path.

Empowerment

Embrace your role as a catalyst for change. The world is eager for your next creation.

Personal achievement

Make the impossible your next project. Your journey leads where others have yet to venture.

Strengths

- **Visionary thinking**: You see opportunities where others see limitations, driving groundbreaking innovations.
- **Action-oriented:** You don't just dream; you do. Your visions have the power to transform entire landscapes.
- **Trendsetting:** You set trends that others follow, positioning yourself as a leader in your field.

Shadow side

- **Overlooking practical details:** Your excitement for innovation can sometimes cause you to miss essential practical considerations.
- **Overly idealistic:** Focusing too much on the big picture can make you appear disconnected from reality or dismissive of existing constraints.
- **Resistance to routine:** Your desire for constant innovation can lead to frustration with routine tasks, challenging your ability to maintain consistency.

THE SAGE

The Sage is a wellspring of wisdom and a beacon of knowledge. Valuing truth and understanding, they often take on roles as mentors, coaches, or strategic advisors. Their insights guide others through uncertainty, lighting the way toward clarity.

Self-discovery

Your wisdom is a powerful gift, and sharing it is your legacy. Your insights illuminate the paths of those around you.

Empowerment

Keep enlightening, teaching, and inspiring. Your words can shift perspectives and drive action.

Personal achievement

Write the books, lead the discussions, and be the mentor who transforms lives. Your thought leadership shapes the world.

Strengths

- **Enlightenment and guidance:** You provide clarity in times of uncertainty, inspiring and teaching those around you.
- **Deep insight:** Your insights influence critical decisions and shift the tides of thought.
- **Strategic thinking:** You excel in planning, often anticipating outcomes and guiding others toward informed choices.

Shadow side

- **Overly critical:** Your high standards may lead to self-criticism or alienate others, potentially stifling creativity.
- **Detached:** A focus on knowledge and truth can make you seem emotionally distant or unapproachable.
- **Analysis paralysis:** Your pursuit of understanding might cause hesitation in decision-making, leading to missed opportunities.

THE CREATOR

The Creator is driven by a deep need to express and bring unique ideas to life. You see the world not just for what it is, but for what it could be, using your imagination to create work that resonates on a deeper level.

Self-discovery

You have a gift for seeing potential where others see limitations. Your creativity turns ideas into realities that inspire and captivate.

Empowerment

Trust your imagination and let it guide you to create things that connect with others on a meaningful level. Your vision lights the way for those around you.

Personal achievement

Bring your ideas to life in ways that captivate and transform. Your creative touch has the power to turn the ordinary into something truly special.

Strengths

- **Endless imagination:** You see possibilities everywhere, and your creativity knows no bounds.
- **Unique expression:** You have a knack for creating work that speaks to universal themes and connects deeply with people.
- **Visionary:** You excel at taking the ordinary and making it extraordinary, turning simple ideas into something impactful.

Shadow side

- **Lost in ideas:** Sometimes, you can get so caught up in your imagination that it's hard to stay grounded and make your ideas a reality.
- **Struggle with follow-through:** While you're great at coming up with ideas, finishing them can be a challenge, leading to frustration or unfinished projects.
- **Perfectionism:** Your desire to create something exceptional can sometimes lead to endless tweaking, preventing you from finishing and sharing your work.

THE PROTECTOR

The Protector is all about nurturing and supporting those around them, creating a safe and caring environment. Your strength lies in your capacity to care deeply and act fiercely, standing tall as a guardian of values and a defender of dreams.

Self-discovery

Your power comes from your ability to care deeply and act with determination. You are a shield and a sanctuary for those in your circle.

Empowerment

Embrace your role as a guardian of values and defender of dreams. Your presence provides comfort, and your actions offer relief.

Personal achievement

Lead initiatives that protect and nurture. Your mission to heal, support, and protect is a calling with profound impact.

Strengths

- **Nurturing and supportive:** You create a safe haven where others can thrive, offering emotional and practical support.
- **Deeply caring:** Your ability to care deeply provides unwavering strength to those around you.
- **Fierce defender:** You stand tall as a protector of values and dreams, ensuring those you care for feel safe and valued.

Shadow side

- **Struggles with boundaries:** You may find it challenging to set boundaries, often taking on too much responsibility or becoming overly involved in others' lives.
- **Overly sensitive:** Your deep empathy can sometimes make you overly sensitive to criticism or the emotions of others, leading to emotional exhaustion.
- **Resistant to change:** In your desire to maintain stability, you may resist necessary changes, potentially hindering growth or progress.

THE PIONEER

The Pioneer is driven by an adventurous spirit, always seeking new challenges and unexplored territories. You thrive on change and innovation, forging paths where none exist. Adventure calls your name, and you answer with gusto; inspiring others to follow and explore beyond the familiar.

Self-discovery

Adventure is your calling, and you embrace it with enthusiasm. Every challenge is an opportunity, and boundaries are mere suggestions.

Empowerment

Forge paths where none exist. Your bold steps inspire others to venture beyond the familiar.

Personal achievement

Be the first, the bravest, the one who dares to dream. Your journeys become legacies of courage and inspiration.

Strengths

- **Embraces change:** You thrive on change and innovation, constantly seeking new challenges and opportunities.
- **Trailblazer:** Your natural ability to forge new paths inspires others to explore beyond their comfort zones.
- **Courageous leadership:** Your adventurous spirit and boldness make you a leader in uncharted territories, setting the pace for others.

Shadow side

- **Perceived as reckless:** Your love for adventure can sometimes be seen as reckless, leading to unnecessary risks.
- **Struggles with consistency:** You may find it challenging to maintain consistency, often moving on to the next challenge before completing the current one.
- **Restlessness:** Your constant drive for new experiences can lead to restlessness, making it difficult to stay grounded or commit to long-term projects.

THE SOVEREIGN

The Sovereign embodies leadership and authority. Decisive and strong-willed, you excel at managing both people and resources. Command comes naturally, and leadership is your role by destiny and achievement.

Self-discovery

Command and respect come naturally to you. Leadership is your destiny, shaped by both your inherent qualities and your achievements.

Empowerment

Guide, govern, and grow with a steady hand and a clear vision. Your decisions chart the course for others to follow.

Personal achievement

Aim for the pinnacle; it is your rightful place. Lead with authority, and let your legacy be one of success and inspiration.

Strengths

- **Decisive leadership:** You guide, govern, and grow with clarity and confidence, setting a course that others willingly follow.
- **Commanding presence:** Your natural authority earns respect, enabling you to manage people and resources effectively.
- **Strategic vision:** You possess a strong strategic vision, steering your team or organization towards sustained success and growth.

Shadow side

- **Overly controlling:** You may become overly controlling, struggling to relinquish authority or consider input from others.
- **Difficulty delegating:** A reluctance to delegate can lead to burnout, as you might believe that only you can ensure tasks are done correctly.
- **Risk of isolation:** Your strong-willed nature and focus on authority can sometimes isolate you from your team, making collaboration and open communication challenging.

THE MAVERICK

The Maverick is unconventional and independent, constantly challenging norms and pushing boundaries. Fearless in the face of tradition, you stand alone if necessary to bring about essential change.

Self-discovery

Unconventional and unyielding, you reshape the world to align with your vision. Standards are yours to set, and limits are yours to defy.

Empowerment

Continue to challenge the status quo. Your unique perspective isn't just needed-it's essential.

Personal achievement

Drive innovation and change. Be the leader who not only thinks differently but dares to make a difference.

Strengths

- **Boundary pusher:** You challenge existing norms, often leading the charge in innovation and necessary change.
- **Independent thinker:** Fiercely independent, you stand alone against tradition or popular opinion to pursue what you believe is right.
- **Change agent:** Your unconventional approach frequently leads to breakthroughs and transformations, reshaping the world according to your vision.

Shadow side

- **Perceived as reckless:** Your willingness to defy norms can sometimes be perceived as reckless, leading others to question your judgment.
- **Struggles with consistency:** Your drive for constant change can lead to inconsistency, making it difficult to maintain long-term commitments or follow through on every idea.
- **Isolation:** Your independent nature and unyielding stance can isolate you from others, making collaboration challenging and potentially leading to conflicts.

THE HEALER

The Healer is committed to harmony and wellness, promoting healing in all forms – physical, emotional, and social. Your presence acts as a balm, restoring balance and peace wherever you go.

Self-discovery

Your touch naturally heals, bringing peace and balance to a chaotic world. You are a source of calm, nurturing the spaces and souls around you.

Empowerment

Envision your healing ability becoming a beacon for those seeking solace and strength. Your journey is about transforming environments and relationships, not just healing.

Personal achievement

Create sanctuaries of health and happiness wherever you go. Your efforts mend lives, strengthening each community you touch.

Strengths

- **Restores balance:** You bring peace and wellness to those around you, whether in physical, emotional, or social contexts.
- **Nurturing presence:** Your calming presence serves as a source of comfort and stability, especially in times of stress or chaos.
- **Transformative impact:** You have the ability to foster harmony and wellness, transforming environments and relationships in every space you touch.

Shadow side

- **Overly sensitive:** Your deep empathy can sometimes lead you to absorb the emotions and stress of others, which can become overwhelming.
- **Struggles with boundaries:** Your desire to help may make it difficult to set boundaries, risking burnout or emotional exhaustion.
- **Avoidance of conflict:** In pursuing harmony, you might avoid necessary conflicts, potentially allowing issues to fester rather than addressing them head-on.

THE CONNECTOR

The Connector excels in building relationships and networks. You have an innate ability to bring people together, fostering strong partnerships and creating collaborative opportunities.

Self-discovery

You are the thread that weaves through the fabric of communities, turning strangers into allies and synergies into movements.

Empowerment

Envision yourself at the heart of a vibrant network where every connection multiplies opportunities and deepens understanding. Your interactions don't just build bridges-they turn networks into powerful catalysts for change.

Personal achievement

Lead initiatives where your ability to connect is the cornerstone of success. Every relationship you cultivate sparks new ideas, drives innovation, and creates enduring partnerships that leave lasting legacies.

Strengths

- **Relationship builder:** You excel at building strong, lasting partnerships, effortlessly bringing people together.
- **Community catalyst:** Your talent for connecting people creates powerful synergies, fostering collaboration and innovation within communities.
- **Bridge-builder:** You uniquely build bridges across different groups and ideas, creating networks that are both extensive and deeply impactful.

Shadow side

- **Spreads themselves too thin:** Your drive to maintain many relationships may lead to burnout or reduced effectiveness.
- **Perceived as superficial:** A focus on networking might sometimes come across as superficial if deeper relationships aren't cultivated.
- **Difficulty with depth:** While you excel at creating connections, maintaining deeper, more meaningful relationships over time can be challenging, risking the loss of genuine bonds.

THE ADVENTURER

The Adventurer is driven by exploration, spontaneity, and a zest for life. Thriving in dynamic environments, they constantly seek new experiences and challenges, often leading others by example with their fearless approach to life.

Self-discovery

You are a trailblazer, unafraid to venture into the unknown. Your curiosity drives you to discover new paths and possibilities, inspiring others to follow in your footsteps.

Empowerment

Embrace your role as the catalyst for excitement and change. Your adventures ignite the spark in others, encouraging them to embark on their own journeys.

Personal achievement

Push your boundaries and explore uncharted territories. Your life is a series of thrilling quests, each more exciting than the last, leaving behind a legacy of bravery and inspiration.

Strengths

- **Zest for life:** Your enthusiasm and fearlessness inspire those around you to embrace new experiences and challenges.
- **Curiosity-driven:** Your insatiable curiosity leads you to explore uncharted territories, uncovering new possibilities that others might overlook.
- **Trailblazer:** You set an example of courage and spontaneity, motivating others to step out of their comfort zones.

The shadow side

- **Impulsiveness:** Your love for spontaneity can sometimes lead to impulsive decisions, resulting in unforeseen consequences.
- **Struggles with stability:** Your constant need for new experiences can make it difficult to settle down or maintain stability in your personal or professional life.
- **Difficulty with long-term Commitment:** Your desire for novelty can lead to challenges in committing to long-term projects or relationships, potentially leaving things unfinished.

Embracing your archetype

Understanding your Personal Brand Archetype is just the beginning. The next step is to fully embrace it and use it to your advantage. This means highlighting your strengths in your branding and marketing efforts while being mindful of your potential pitfalls.

For example, as an Innovator, you might focus on sharing your big ideas with your audience, inspiring them with your vision. But you'll also need to ensure you have a solid team in place to handle the practical aspects and keep everything running smoothly.

If you're a Protector, your brand might emphasise community and support, making your clients feel valued and cared for. But be aware of setting boundaries to avoid burnout and ensure you're taking care of yourself as well.

Putting it all together

Your Personal Brand Archetype is a powerful tool that can help you create a more authentic and effective brand. By understanding and embracing your archetype, you can communicate more clearly with your audience, build stronger connections, and stand out in your industry.

Take some time to reflect on your archetype and how it shows up in your business. Journal about your strengths and potential pitfalls, and brainstorm ways to leverage your unique traits to stand out from the crowd. Remember, your archetype is not a box to confine you but a framework to guide you towards greater authenticity and success.

As you integrate your archetype into your personal brand, reflect on your unique traits and how they can be showcased to create a compelling and authentic connection with your audience. This question will guide you in aligning your brand with your true self, making your interactions more impactful and meaningful:

"How can I use my personal brand essence to stand out and connect deeply with my audience?"

CHAPTER 4

DARE TO BE DIFFERENT

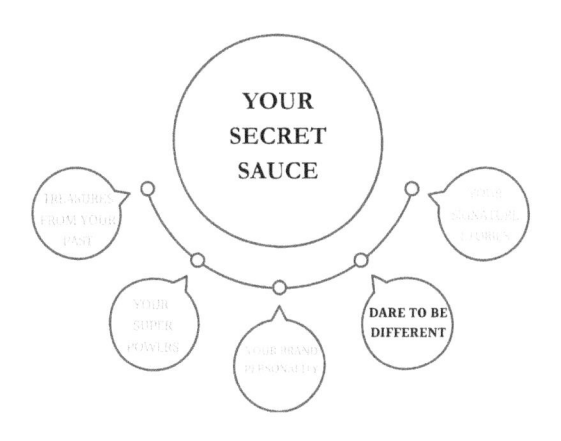

Doing my research for this chapter reminded me of a story from my past that I had forgotten. Way back when I started designing fashion collections, I had a concession in a designer store that held seasonal fashion shows. Each season, as I was designing my collection, my anxiety would go through the roof.

What if my vision isn't understood?

What if being different backfires?

What if the collection is a flop and nobody buys it?

I remember thinking how each new collection was like sticking your head out and risking getting it lobbed off. But here's the thing, I never lost my head. I felt the anxiety, but I didn't die. The right people understood, and those who didn't get it, well, I learned to not worry about them. Over the years, the fear faded because I attracted my tribe, and they became loyal to my brand. Each season, I would ship the collection to the stores, and the day the boxes landed, I'd always get phone calls for re-orders because the collections sold right out of the box-they never even made it onto the rails. That was the power in focusing on the people who love what you do.

Being different is your biggest asset

Being willing to stand out from the crowd takes courage. It's not for the faint of heart. It can be terrifying, but every time you take a risk, you learn and grow. Do it a few times and you will get ballsier and soon fear will be replaced by braver and bolder moves forward. Do this one thing alone, and you will stand out from the crowd. Being a visual person, I like to think of it as going off-piste and having all that fresh snow to yourself. Following your own vision allows you to step away from your competition.

Stories of iconic figures

Throughout history, the most well-known personal brand owners have stood out from the crowd by embracing their unique visions and daring to be different. They didn't just follow trends; they set them. They leaned into their values and beliefs and built their entire brand on them. By doing so, they attracted their tribe – people who resonated deeply with their message and vision. These iconic figures understood that the key to their success was not in blending in but in standing out, often at great personal risk. Their stories serve as powerful examples of how leaning into your uniqueness and daring to be different can lead to immense success and lasting impact.

Brené Brown

A researcher and storyteller, Brené dared to be different by tackling the uncomfortable topics of vulnerability and shame. Her TED Talk, "The Power of Vulnerability," went viral, challenging conventional norms about strength and leadership. By embracing vulnerability herself, Brown has inspired millions to lead more authentic and courageous lives.

Ellen Degeneres

Ellen made a bold move by coming out as gay in the 1990s, a decision that had significant professional repercussions at the time. However, her authenticity and courage eventually led to a highly successful career as a talk show host and comedian. Ellen's story highlights the power of staying true to oneself and the positive impact it can have in the long run.

Lady Gaga

Lady Gaga is an artist who has consistently pushed the boundaries of music, fashion, and performance. Her willingness to take risks and embrace her unique style has garnered her a massive following and critical acclaim. Gaga's journey underscores the importance of authenticity and the impact of daring to be different in the entertainment industry.

Ruth Bader Ginsburg

As a towering figure in the fight for gender equality, Ruth demonstrated remarkable resilience and determination throughout her career. Appointed as the second woman ever to the U.S. Supreme Court, she tirelessly championed women's rights and civil liberties. Her landmark opinions and dissents have left an indelible mark on American jurisprudence. Beyond her legal legacy, Ginsburg's tenacity and courage have made her an enduring icon of strength and perseverance.

The power of having a point of view

One of the most powerful ways to dare to be different is by embracing and expressing your unique point of view. In a noisy world where everyone is competing for attention, having a clear, unapologetic perspective is what sets you apart and magnetises the right people to you. But standing out doesn't mean you have to weigh in on every topic under the sun. True power lies in the deliberate choice of where you invest your voice and energy.

You get to decide what you stand for and what you are known for. This isn't about being loud; it's about being intentional. It's about knowing your core beliefs and values, and having the courage to stand by them, even when they challenge the status quo. Your point of view becomes a beacon for those who resonate with your message, drawing them in not just because of what you say, but because of how deeply you believe in it.

Being unapologetic about your point of view means owning your truth without fear of rejection or judgment. It's about understanding that your voice has the power to inspire, provoke, and create change – when used with intention and purpose. You're not here to please everyone, and that's exactly what makes your voice so potent. You're here to make a difference, to champion ideas that matter to you, and to impact your industry in a way that only you can.

So, as you think about how you want to use your voice, consider these questions to help you refine and solidify your point of view:

- What are the beliefs you can put energy behind?
- What inspires you and fills you with passion?
- What pisses you off?
- What unique perspective do you bring to your industry?
- How can your personal experiences shape your point of view?
- What values are non-negotiable for you?
- What change do you want to see in your field?
- How can you use your story to connect with others authentically?
- Your authentic voice is your most powerful tool. And remember, you can build your whole brand on one powerful belief.

Overcoming the fear of standing out

Standing out can be terrifying, especially when you're venturing into uncharted territory. It's natural to fear judgement, rejection, or failure. However, overcoming this fear is crucial to unlocking your full potential. Start by acknowledging your fear and understanding that it's a common experience for anyone pushing boundaries. Embrace your individuality and remember that your unique perspective is what makes you valuable. Surround yourself with a supportive tribe that encourages and uplifts you. Practice self-compassion and give yourself permission to take risks and make mistakes. Each step you take outside your comfort zone strengthens your resilience and builds confidence. Ultimately, the rewards of daring to be different far outweigh the temporary discomfort of standing out. Embrace your uniqueness, and let it be the driving force that propels you towards your greatest achievements.

Whenever you face a challenging decision or feel the pull of fear holding you back let this question push you to take bold actions that align with your highest self and true purpose:

"What would courageous me do?"

By consistently choosing courage over comfort, you'll pave the way to remarkable growth and impact.

CHAPTER 5

YOUR SIGNATURE STORIES

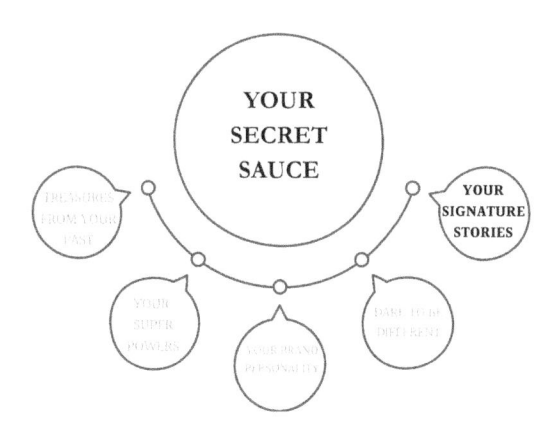

Story #1: Pivoting away from the edge

I've pivoted several times in my business, often from the edge of a cliff– metaphorically speaking. There were at least three times I should have gone crashing over that cliff, but I managed to create new directions and avoid disaster. Being the sole provider for my three kids drove me to find solutions and innovate continuously. In my fashion business, I've done retail, wholesale, distribution, pop-ups, a luxury department store concession, my own stores and e-commerce. Some of these overlapped, and at the time, they felt like natural next steps rather than major pivots. Looking back, I see the hair-raising moments that could have ended it all. It's those very experiences that empower me to dream bigger and relentlessly pursue the impossible.

Story #2: Cody's revival

My client Cody Burch is also my marketing coach. He closed his own business in 2022 to take up a dream job offer with one of his favourite clients. Six months later, he lost that job. He started January 2023 with no clients and no income. Cody's saving grace was that even though he thought he had closed his business forever, he kept emailing his list every day. You see, Cody is a master storyteller. Once Cody made the announcement that he had lost his job, people started reaching out to him asking for his help. Within a few weeks, Cody was back in business, building it stronger and faster than ever before. His email list saved him.

Story #3: Playing the long game

My coach Rich Litvin started coaching 16 years ago from a beach in Thailand, where he was travelling after losing his teaching job. His first client paid him $10 a month. He was thrilled because he had only ever been paid for teaching, and this client was paying him just to talk to him. Rich uses this story to inspire his coaching clients to see building their coaching practice as a long game, one built on one powerful conversation at a time.

Story #4: Braver together

Diane Cunningham Ellis is my business bestie. We talk all day long, even though she is on the other side of the world. Diane runs a mastermind called Braver Together, and she is the queen of brave. Diane weaves her signature stories around being brave into everything she does, attracting her ideal clients. From surviving a plane crash to divorce to being in recovery, her stories of bravery and resilience inspire her clients to step into their brave too.

Story #5: Creating order out of chaos

I am a minimalist. Whether it's curating my fashion collections, detoxing my home, creating processes for my business, or helping my clients achieve their impossible, I look for ways to create simplicity. I love creating order out of chaos, making things light and easy. When I closed my stores and transitioned to an e-commerce business model, I kept asking myself, "How can I make this light and easy?" This approach helped me create a streamlined business that generates 84% of the income I had with two stores in just a few hours each week … without the overheads of a brick and mortar business.

The power of signature stories

Harnessing and sharing your signature stories is one of the most powerful tools you have to connect with and impact your clients. Your unique experiences and the lessons you've learned along the way are what set you apart and make you relatable. When you share these stories, you not only humanise your brand, you also build trust and authenticity. Signature stories help you illustrate your journey, showcase your resilience, and highlight your expertise in a way that resonates deeply with your clients.

Your signature stories offer a unique point of difference and reveal why you are who you are. They illustrate what led you to where you are today and why you are passionate about your work. These stories are the essence of your personal brand, and they create a deep connection with your audience. They make you relatable, memorable, and inspiring. Reflect on how each story you tell adds value to your clients and how it aligns with your brand message.

Standing out from the noise

If you are not standing out from the noise, you are either adding to it, or you are invisible. Curating meaningful signature stories that resonate with your ideal clients makes you memorable and frees you from the content creation hamster wheel. Your signature stories anchor your brand and give you a solid foundation to build on. They guide your content creation, ensuring that everything you share aligns with your core message and values.

Now it's over to you. What are some of your signature stories? Here are 20 story mining prompts…. With these ideas, you can start identifying and crafting your signature stories that will resonate deeply with your audience. These stories will not only highlight your unique journey but also create a strong, relatable connection with those you aim to inspire and lead.

Extracting your signature stories

Defining moments

Reflect on the moments that significantly impacted your life or career. What experiences shaped who you are today? Example: A life-changing event that altered your perspective.

Overcoming challenges

Share stories of obstacles you faced and how you overcame them. These can inspire and motivate others facing similar challenges. Example: A time when you turned a failure into a stepping stone.

Successes and achievements

Highlight key achievements and what you learned from those successes. Make them valuable. Focus on how you achieved them, and the insights you got along the way. Example: Winning a prestigious award and the journey that led to it.

Failures and lessons learned

Don't shy away from sharing failures. These stories often contain valuable lessons, show your resilience and empower others to embrace their failures as stepping stones to greater things ahead. Example: A time you went against your gut instinct and paid the price!?

Aha moments

Recall times when you had a sudden realisation or breakthrough. What led to this moment, and how did it change your perspective? What advice or tips do you have for others

THE MAGNETIC FEMALE ENTREPRENEUR

who are looking for their own breakthroughs? Example: A moment of clarity that redirected your career path.

Passion projects

Talk about projects or initiatives you are passionate about. What drives you to pursue them, and what impact have they had? These stories help your future clients to connect with your why. Example: A charitable project that aligns with your values.

Personal values

Identify stories that highlight your core values. How have these values guided your decisions and actions? Example: A decision guided by your commitment to integrity.

Inspirational figures

Share stories of people who have inspired you. How did they influence your journey? What lessons did you learn from them? Example: A mentor who provided pivotal advice at a crucial moment.

Turning points

Focus on pivotal moments that led to significant change or redirection in your life or career. What led to them, how did it feel going through them, how did things look different on the other side? Example: A career change that opened new opportunities.

Behind-the-scenes

Give a glimpse into your process, whether it's behind the scenes of your business, your creative process, or your daily routine. (This one activity, on its own was the reason why my business survived the covid pandemic when our stores were forced to close.) Example: The daily habits that keep you productive and focused.

Client success stories

Highlight the successes of your clients or those you've helped. How did you contribute to their achievements? My coach Daniel Priestley taught me this one. It was a game changer for me "You don't have to be *in* the spotlight, you can *be* the spotlight" Example: A client who achieved remarkable results through your guidance.

Lessons from mentors

Share advice or lessons you received from mentors and how they've influenced your path. Be generous in acknowledging the input from others in your journey to success. Example: A piece of wisdom that has been a guiding principle in your life.

Personal anecdotes

Simple, relatable stories from your everyday life that reveal something about your character or philosophy. Be sure to tie the story into something of value for your audience, otherwise, you are just adding to the noise. Example: A personal habit that has had a significant impact on your well-being.

Cultural and background influences

How has your cultural background or upbringing shaped your perspective and approach? These add to the uniqueness of your journey and help your audience to connect with you on a deeper level. Example: A family tradition that has influenced your values.

Moments of courage

Times when you took a significant risk or made a bold decision. What was the outcome? Share with vulnerability but include the lessons learned or it is just public therapy. Example: Leaving a secure job to pursue your passion.

Career highlights

Key milestones in your professional journey that define your career. Sprinkle these with other forms of content as sharing content that is just a highlight reel of your successes is not the best way to build deeper connections. Example: The launch of a successful product or service.

Unexpected twists

Surprising turns in your journey that led to unexpected but valuable outcomes. These stories are juicy, and people love them! Example: A serendipitous event that opened new doors.

Long-term goals

Stories about your big dreams and long-term goals. If you don't want to share specifics, consider sharing about your bigger vision, mission, or desired impact. Example: A vision for the future and the steps you're taking to achieve it.

Community involvement

Stories about your involvement in the community or causes you care about. Example: Volunteering efforts that reflect your commitment to social responsibility.

Personal growth

Reflect on your personal development journey. What habits, routines, or practices have contributed to your growth? Example: A self-care routine that has significantly improved your mental health.

Content buckets

You can also use your story-mining expedition to decide on what content buckets you will create for your business. Content buckets are specific themes or categories that your content will fall into. Three buckets are ideal; five is also good. Less is better. Have as many as you need but not more. Your buckets help you decide what to create content around and what to ditch.

When it comes to creating content, ask yourself these questions:

"What is the value in this story?"

CHAPTER 6

THE SECRET SAUCE FINDER

By now, you've explored your past experiences, uncovered your top strengths, and reflected on your personal brand archetype. You've journaled, reflected, and started to piece together the puzzle of what makes you uniquely powerful. Now it's time to pull it all together.

The Secret Sauce Finder is a tool designed to help you visualize and clarify the core elements that set you apart. It's not just about listing your strengths or passions-it's about understanding how they intersect and create the foundation of your unique brilliance. This is where you go from being "just another option" to being irreplaceable.

Think of it like this: if you zoom out and take a look at the bigger picture of your journey, your experiences, and your strengths, you'll start to see patterns emerge. At the intersection of these elements is where your **secret sauce** lives – the zone where you operate at your highest level, the place where your passion, strength, and experience collide to create something only **you** can offer. This is your superpower, your differentiator, your magic.

Time to reflect and unpack

As you reflect on the first five chapters, take a moment to pause and really consider the following:

- **Treasures from the past:** What experiences, challenges, and victories have shaped who you are today? What lessons have been the most powerful in your journey? These are more than just memories – they are the threads of your secret sauce.

- **Your superpowers:** What are the innate strengths you lean on when times get tough or when you're in flow? These are not just skills – they are the core of what makes you unstoppable.

- **Your *Personal Brand Archetype*:** How does your unique brand personality show up in your business? Whether you're a connector, a nurturer, or an innovator, this part of your secret sauce is the energy that draws people in and makes them want to be a part of what you're creating.

- **Dare to Be Different:** Where are you daring to step outside the norm? What makes you stand out? Your courage to be different is a critical ingredient in your secret sauce.

- **Your Signature Stories:** What stories from your journey speak to your resilience, your strength, and your mission? These stories aren't just about your past. They shape how people see you, trust you, and connect with why you do what you do and buy into your mission.

Bringing it all together

Now it's time to plot these elements using the **Secret Sauce Finder** Venn diagram. Play with this for a while; plot what you think your top three unique elements are and how they intersect. Let yourself experiment and zoom out again, going higher level each time, until you land on the highest-level version of your secret sauce. I had to go through this process several times before I landed on my top three: **innovation, empowerment,** and **relentless execution.**

When you see this clearly, it's like finding the key that unlocks your next level of growth, impact, and influence.

THE SECRET SAUCE FINDER

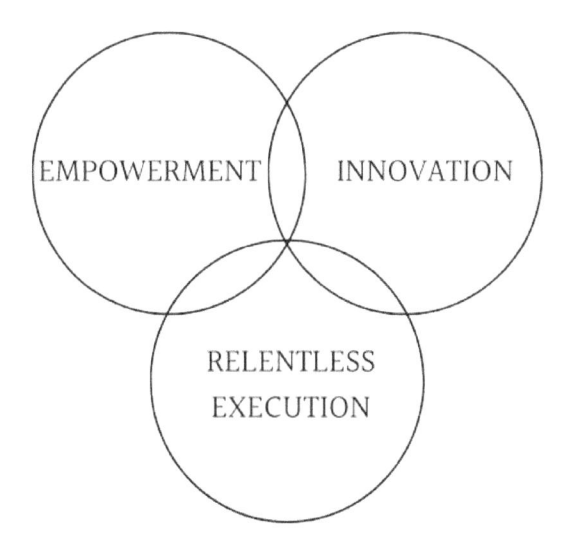

Share and collaborate

Don't keep this discovery to yourself – share it. Ask your colleagues, friends, and family to do the same exercise and exchange feedback. You might be surprised by what others see in you that you might have overlooked. Reflecting on this with others helps you refine your secret sauce even further and may uncover additional strengths and insights.

Your Secret Sauce Finder isn't just a tool – it's a window into the most powerful version of you. Once you've unpacked these elements, everything you create, offer, and build will be grounded in your unique brilliance, making you unstoppable in your next chapter.

BE MAGNETIC

PART 2

BE MAGNETIC

If you've already nailed down the ONE BIG THING you want to be known for, you're ahead of the game. But if you're still searching, don't worry — I'm here to guide you through it. In this section, we're going to either solidify that vision and make it even more expansive, or we're going to help you bravely stake your claim on the world stage.

The truth is, the most inspired and energised version of you creates a magnetic energy that draws people in. It's not just about what you do – it's about who you are when you're fully aligned with your vision. That kind of energy is contagious, it's powerful, and it's the key to attracting the right opportunities, clients, and collaborators into your orbit.

When my clients come to me, ready to level up and create the impact they know they're destined for, I ask them one simple, yet powerful question: *"If you had to burn it all down, what would you grab first?"* It's a question that strips away the noise and gets to the heart of what truly matters. It reveals the biggest, hairiest, scariest goal you hardly dare to imagine-the one that sets your soul on fire.

This is the vision you need to pursue. It's the North Star that will guide every decision, every step, and every evolution of you. It's time to get focused, to embrace the boldness that lives inside you, and to make your mark in a way that only you can. Let's dive into the evolution of you that will catapult you toward that audacious vision, creating a magnetic presence that draws everything you need toward you.

CHAPTER 7

WHAT DO YOU WANT TO BE KNOWN FOR?

Let me be real with you-there have been times when I've been intentional about what I'm known for, and times when I've just let it happen. Spoiler alert: letting it happen doesn't always work out the way you would like it to. You can find yourself in a place you never intended, asking yourself 'how the heck did I end up here??' When I allowed others to define my brand for me, it took years of being stuck in a place I didn't want to be and a monumental amount of willpower to get back on track to where I wanted to be...

Here's how it happened…

In the early days of my fashion business, I had a distinct style. I was known for a specific look-monochrome, quirky, timeless. I didn't follow trends; I created my own tribe of loyal customers who couldn't wait to see what I did next. Then, life threw me a curveball and I had to refocus on what I could do closer to home. Today, this wouldn't be a problem because we have global reach. But back then, it meant making some hard choices.

Instead of sticking with the path that was working, I took a detour. I went wide when I should have gone deep. Serving a domestic audience, I introduced more diversity into my collections. In a moment of non-strategic creativity, I introduced colour – not subtle hues, but vibrant hot pinks, aquas, and purples, sometimes mixing them together. It was a riot, and fun ... for a while. My customers loved it, and because I've always valued feedback, I ran with it. But after a few seasons of playing with colours, I realized something – I was over it. But my customers weren't. I found myself trapped, delivering things I didn't love, allowing others to dictate my brand identity.

Then COVID hit, and my stores closed. Suddenly, I had the opportunity to redefine my brand and step back into my authentic identity. Today, I stand 100% firm in what my fashion brand represents – timeless, wardrobe-building collections for stylish, individual women. It took a lot of strength, courage, and determination to take back ownership of my vision, especially when many of my customers resisted the change. But now, I have a crystal-clear vision of what I stand for, and I'm fiercely loyal to it. I've created filters that keep me on track while still allowing for creative expression.

It took 12 months to reclaim the reins and redefine my brand. What kept me moving forward despite the resistance? A clear vision. Having a clear vision helps you stay on track, create filters, and rule out anything that doesn't align with that vision.

Define or be defined

In the entrepreneurial world, it's all too easy to let others define your brand for you. If you're not actively shaping your identity and message, the world will gladly do it for you-and not always in a way that reflects who you truly are. This can leave you with a brand that feels off, like wearing someone else's shoes that just don't fit.

The beauty of defining your own brand is that it allows you to create something that's authentically you. When you take charge of your narrative, you attract the right clients, align with your values, and feel genuinely fulfilled by the work you do. You're not just another face in the crowd – you're the one setting the tone and leading with what matters most to you.

When you actively define your brand, you're steering the ship. You get to decide how you're perceived, where your business is headed, and what kind of impact you want to make. It's about being proactive rather than reactive, staying true to yourself, even when it feels a little uncomfortable. The payoff? A brand that not only resonates with your audience but also feels right to you.

Sure, the process of defining your brand can be challenging. It takes some introspection and a good dose of courage to stand out from the crowd. But by doing so, you take control of your story, ensuring that your brand reflects your vision and attracts the right opportunities. It's all about being true to yourself and leading with clarity, confidence, and impact.

Let's dive into some of the common challenges you might face when trying to define what you want to be known for, and how to navigate them.

The challenges of defining your brand

Already known for something but want to pivot

Transitioning from one established identity to another can be tricky, especially when people already associate you with something specific. Think of pivoting as evolving your brand rather than abandoning it. This approach allows you to build on your existing reputation while gradually introducing new aspects of your identity. By carefully blending the old with the new, you maintain continuity and credibility, making it easier for your audience to accept and embrace the change.

Perceptions from others

While it's easy to get caught up in how others view you, remember that their perspectives are often shaped by incomplete information or outdated assumptions. People's perceptions might be off because they've known a previous version of you or because you've shown up to please others. It's time to be unapologetic about who you are and what you want. Get clear on where you are going, then focus on your vision, goals and who you need to be moving forward.

Lack of clarity

Not being clear about where you're going can lead to confusion and inconsistency in your brand. Aim to be rooted in your values, goals, and vision. When your vision is clear, it provides a strong foundation for your brand, helping you make decisions that align with your long-term goals. Clarity acts as a compass, guiding your actions and messaging, ensuring that everything you do is consistent and purposeful.

Fear of judgment

Worrying about how others will perceive your changes can hold you back from making necessary adjustments. Replace the fear of judgment with curiosity and see feedback as a chance to refine and improve. Instead of letting potential criticism paralyse you, view it as valuable insight that can help you grow. Curiosity opens the door to learning and innovation, allowing you to make informed decisions that align with your true path.

Competing visions

Balancing what you're currently known for with what you aspire to be known for can be a challenge, especially when you're torn between different possible directions. Now that you've explored your "secret sauce" – those unique strengths and passions that define you – it's time to use this insight to guide your decisions. Whenever you are torn between two or more possible directions, revisit the common thread that ties your past, present, and future together. This thread often points directly to your core strengths or passions, providing a clear path forward. With this clarity, you can ditch distractions and focus on what will truly propel you to the next level.

Resistance to change

People often resist change, both within themselves and from those around them. But change is inevitable. The quicker you get on board with it the better! Getting comfortable with change allows you to view it as a natural part of breaking out of your comfort zone and into your growth zone. When others resist your new direction, it's often because they're accustomed to the version of you they've known. Understand that this resistance is more about their comfort than your potential. Stay grounded in your vision, knowing that over time, as you stay consistent and true to your path, others will either come to accept your new direction or reveal themselves as not aligned with your journey (and that's fine).

Inconsistent messaging

If your messaging is inconsistent, it can confuse your audience and dilute your brand. Ensure that all your communication reflects your brand values and vision. Consistency in messaging builds trust and clarity, helping your audience easily understand who you are and what you stand for.

Overwhelming choices

With so many options available, it can be overwhelming to choose the right path. Narrow down your focus to what truly aligns with your vision and strengths. By homing in on the choices that align with your core values and passions, you simplify the decision-making process and reduce the noise that can lead to confusion.

External pressures

Family, friends, and societal expectations can pressure you into conforming to a path that doesn't align with your true self. It's important to stay true to your own values and vision. Acknowledge these influences, but don't let them dictate your direction. Staying true to yourself requires clarity and courage, especially when those around you may not fully understand your choices.

Stagnation

Failing to evolve can lead to stagnation. Continuously seek opportunities for growth and innovation to stay relevant and dynamic. The landscape around you is always changing, and by actively pursuing new ideas, you keep your brand fresh and engaging.

Stepping into a bigger vision

When I set out on my adventures as a coach and strategic thinking partner, I knew I wanted to have more impact in the world than just making my clients feel good in their clothes. It felt like the next logical step to me, even if it didn't make sense to people who knew me as a designer. Even though I wasn't completely sure where I was going, I took the steps. The first revealed the next, and the next revealed the one after. From there, I just allowed the journey to unfold.

Sometimes you need to travel the journey for a while, following your instincts, before the bigger vision reveals itself. At times, you might need to clear space in your life or business to allow that vision to come into focus. That's exactly what I was doing when I closed my coaching membership at the end of 2023. One of my top strengths is being a relator; I thrive on deep relationships, so the hardest part of letting that membership go was leaving the people behind. But, I knew that to create space for my next chapter, something had to give.

I took the next six months to let my vision unfold while having dozens of one-on-one conversations with the people I ideally wanted to work with: female entrepreneurs. I knew that I wanted to help women turn their boldest dreams into reality and to stop waiting until the time was right-because the time is never right. These one-on-one conversations helped me see the biggest challenges my ideal clients face and to stay focused on them as I clarified my bigger vision.

Clarity comes from taking action

It can be scary letting something go to make space for the next thing, especially if you're not 100% sure what the next thing looks like. If you are at a fork in the road, undecided about your next steps, I would highly encourage you to start moving, even if you make some missteps-clarity comes from taking action, not from trying to figure out all the steps in your head.

Journaling exercise

To help you navigate these challenges, it's essential to take a step back and reflect on what you truly want to be known for. Journaling is a powerful tool for gaining clarity and setting intentions.

Grab your journal and consider these prompts:

What do I want to be known for?

Reflect on your core values, passions, and the impact you want to make. Consider what legacy you want to leave and how you want your work to resonate with others. This is about defining the essence of your brand and what sets you apart in your field.

How do I want people to perceive me?

Think about the qualities and attributes you want to be associated with your name. Consider how your actions, communication, and presentation influence others' perceptions. Ask yourself how you can consistently embody these qualities in every interaction.

What steps can I take to align my actions with my desired brand identity?

Consider both long and short-term actions that will move you closer to embodying your brand. This might include developing new skills, adjusting your messaging, or taking on projects that reflect your true vision. It's about creating a strategic plan that supports your growth.

What fears or doubts are holding me back from fully embracing my desired identity?

Acknowledge these feelings and think about how to address them. Understanding the roots of your fears can help you develop strategies to overcome them. Consider how reframing these doubts and taking small, confident steps can gradually build your belief in your ability to succeed.

Who can support me?

Identify mentors, coaches, or peers who can provide guidance and encouragement. Surround yourself with people who understand your goals and can offer valuable insights or feedback. These supporters should be individuals who not only believe in your potential but also challenge you to grow and stay accountable. Consider reaching out to those who have walked a similar path or who possess the expertise you need to move forward.

Whenever you find yourself feeling overwhelmed by what others are doing or think you should be doing, ask yourself:

"Does this bring me closer to my vision, or am I doing this because I think I should?"

CHAPTER 8

ONE DEGREE PIVOT

Rossbeigh, Kerry - Newfoundland

Rossbeigh, Kerry - **Puerto** Rico

Last week, I found myself on Rossbeigh beach, on the rugged coast of Kerry, Ireland. Sitting there, facing the vast expanse of the Atlantic Ocean, I couldn't help but wonder: If I were to set sail straight across this ocean, where would I end up? Curiosity got the better of me, and with the help of my GPS, I discovered that a straight line from where I sat would take me to Newfoundland, Canada.

But then I thought, what if I turned just one degree to the west? I made the tiniest adjustment, barely noticeable. My destination changed completely. According to my GPS, I'd now land in Puerto Rico instead of Canada. It was a tiny shift, just one degree, but it altered my course entirely.

This simple, almost whimsical experiment got me thinking about the power of a one-degree pivot in business and in life. So often, we think that to create meaningful change, we need to overhaul everything – change careers, rebrand entirely, or uproot our lives. But sometimes, all we need is a one-degree pivot. Just a small, deliberate shift in direction can take us to a completely different place.

In business, this can be as simple as focusing more on impact, tweaking how you show up to grow your influence, tweaking your product offerings, shifting your target market slightly, or changing your messaging by a fraction. In life, it could be a small change in routine, a slight adjustment in your mindset, or a new perspective on an old problem. These are tiny pivots that can be made in a moment, that over time can lead you to a destination you never imagined.

The beauty of the one-degree pivot is that it doesn't require you to abandon everything you've built or start from scratch. It's about recognizing that even the smallest changes can have a profound impact when compounded over time. It's a reminder that you don't need to overhaul your life to move in a new direction. Sometimes, a small adjustment is all it takes to set you on a path to extraordinary outcomes.

So, the next time you find yourself feeling stuck or in need of change, before you do anything drastic, ask yourself:

What's the one-degree pivot you can make today that might lead to a completely different tomorrow?

CHAPTER 9

THE EVOLUTION OF YOU

Every new chapter in your life or business requires you to evolve, but that doesn't mean you have to overhaul everything overnight. Sometimes, the most powerful transformations come from making small, intentional changes consistently over time. These small shifts compound and lead to significant growth, helping you to step into the next version of yourself with ease and confidence.

Visualize the person you want to become-the version of you who has already achieved the goals you're working toward. What small habits, beliefs, or practices does this future version of you embody? What could you start doing today that aligns you more closely with this vision?

This isn't about rejecting who you are now; it's about gradually stepping into a more empowered, intentional version of yourself. The next-level you is already within you, waiting to be uncovered. By focusing on small, manageable changes, you can begin to shed old habits and mindsets that no longer serve you and adopt new ones that align with your bigger vision.

This process is about being deliberate with your growth. It's not about rushing to the finish line but rather about making steady progress in a way that feels right to you. As you make these shifts, you'll start to notice that you're not just achieving more – you're doing it in a way that feels authentic and sustainable. This is the foundation of true, lasting success.

Introducing the MG Magnetic Matrix

Success isn't just about knowing what to do-it's about aligning what you're doing with who you're being. You can have all the strategy in the world, but if people can sense you're holding back, if you're not fully lit up by your own mission, they'll feel it. And here's the truth: if you're not connected to that fire inside, nothing else will connect either.

The *MG Magnetic Matrix* is here to remind you that the world doesn't need you to blend in – it needs you to be unapologetically you. That's where the magic happens. People follow passion, not perfection. They don't just buy into what you do, they buy into why you do it. So if you're holding back, trying to stay liked or avoid criticism, you're limiting your potential. Owning your spicy point of view and letting that be the rocket that launches you is the game changer.

Standing out takes courage. There are a hundred reasons to stay small: fear of judgment, fear of criticism, fear of what your friends and family will think. But staying small isn't going to create the impact you crave. Owning your mission, standing up for what you believe in, and sharing it with raw passion-that's what moves people. When you harness what is unique and powerful about you and connect deeply and passionately with your mission and step into the spotlight, even if it makes you squirm, that's when you become magnetic to the people you feel called to work with.

Let's dive into the four quadrants of *The MG Magnetic Matrix* and the unique energy each one holds:

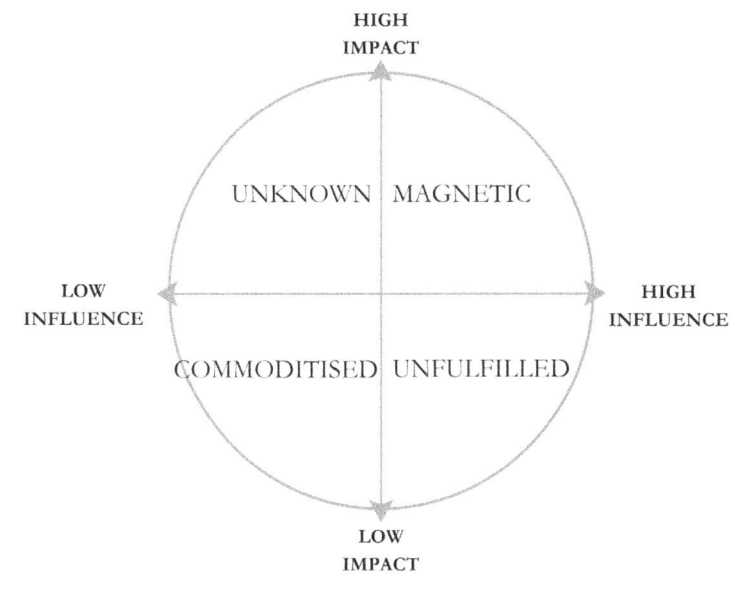

THE MG MAGNETIC MATRIX

COMMODITISED

Playing it safe and staying invisible

In this quadrant, you're working hard but blending in. You're busy, but your efforts aren't generating the recognition or influence you crave. It's not that you're doing the wrong things, but you're not showing up with the energy and presence that makes people take notice. It feels safer to stick with what's expected, to stay under the radar rather than risk stepping out and being seen for what truly sets you apart.

This space is often where we find ourselves when we're playing small, fearing judgment or criticism. You may be focusing on being liked rather than being bold. But the truth is, staying invisible comes at a cost-your unique value is being lost in the noise. To move out of this space, you need to stop hiding. It's not just about taking action – it's about stepping into who you are unapologetically and allowing that energy to shine.

The challenge: Shifting from doing what feels comfortable to fully owning your voice and standing out. You don't need to change everything you're doing – just stop hiding your passion and uniqueness from the world.

UNKNOWN

High impact, but still under the radar

You're already making an impact, but you're like a hidden gem. You're delivering powerful results, but people aren't noticing because you're not stepping up to be seen. Your passion and talent are there, but your visibility is low, and that's holding you back from reaching the next level.

This quadrant is where you can feel frustrated – knowing you're doing incredible work but not getting the recognition you deserve. People don't know you exist because you're not fully embracing visibility. It's not about being loud or flashy; it's about stepping into your space and owning it. The world needs to see what you're capable of, and it's up to you to show them.

The challenge: Moving from being the best-kept secret to being recognized for your work. People respond to energy, so when you show up fully and share your mission with passion, that's when you start to create waves.

UNFULFILLED

You're visible, but something's missing

Here, you've got the spotlight, but it's not lighting you up anymore. You're visible, you're known, but your impact feels hollow. You've achieved success, but it's not aligned with your true passion, leaving you feeling unfulfilled despite the recognition. You might be getting the external validation, but internally, something feels off.

This quadrant can be tricky because it looks like you've "made it" from the outside, but inside, you know you're not doing the work that truly lights you up. You might be stuck doing what's expected rather than what feels deeply aligned. The shift here is about realigning with your mission and reconnecting with the work that fuels your passion. When you lead from that space, you'll find fulfilment and impact in equal measure.

The challenge: Reconnecting with your deeper purpose and aligning your visibility with your true mission. It's about moving from what's expected to what truly drives you and makes your work feel meaningful again.

MAGNETIC

Where your passion and presence are unstoppable

This is the sweet spot. You're showing up fully in your power, aligned with your mission, and letting your passion drive your every move. People are drawn to you because they can feel that you're not just doing the work-you're living it. This is where your influence and impact explode because you're operating from a space of pure alignment and energy.

In this quadrant, you're not chasing opportunities – they're coming to you. You've mastered the balance of doing and being, where your actions are a reflection of who you truly are. Your tribe follows you not just because of what you do, but because of who you are. You've become magnetic, a force that others want to be around, and your impact ripples outward effortlessly.

The challenge: Staying aligned and continuing to evolve. Being magnetic isn't about staying comfortable-it's about continually stepping into new levels of influence and impact. The moment you get complacent, you risk losing that spark. Keep letting your passion lead, and you'll continue to inspire and attract.

The MG Magnetic Matrix isn't about doing more – it's about being more. It's about showing up with the kind of passion that makes people want to be part of your journey. When you step into that fire, that's when everything changes.

Important side note:

If you are like many of my clients and the thought of 'putting yourself out there' is terrifying, think of it like this: you are not **in** the spotlight, you **are** the spotlight. If your mission is not lighting a fire under your ass, keep working it until it does. This one shift alone will catapult you from playing small to a whole new level of impact and influence.

Reflection and action steps

To make the most of The *MG Magnetic Matrix,* here are three steps to help you move into your magnetic power:

1. Get real about where you are

Take a moment to assess your current position in the matrix. Which quadrant are you living in right now? This is about honesty, not judgment. Look at your recent actions, decisions, and the energy you've been bringing to your work. Are you playing it safe, staying invisible, or maybe you're visible but feeling unfulfilled? Write down your reflections – this clarity is the first step to shifting where you need to go.

2. Own what's next

Look at the quadrants and think about where you're headed. What would it look like to fully embody your magnetic power? Visualise it. How does this version of you think, act, and show up in the world? This isn't about perfection – it's about alignment. Identify one key shift that could move you toward stepping into your full, unapologetic power. Let this vision fuel you and guide your next steps.

3. Take bold, aligned action

Now it's time to move. Break down that vision into actionable steps, no matter how small. Whether it's a mindset shift, showing up more visibly, or reconnecting with your mission, make sure every action is aligned with the magnetic version of you. Keep things simple, but stay consistent. The more you show up in alignment, the more magnetic you become.

Whenever you feel yourself holding back, ask yourself:

Am I stepping fully into my magnetic presence?

This question can realign you with your passion and purpose whenever doubt or distractions arise.

CHAPTER 10

FOLLOW YOUR NORTH STAR

In the entrepreneurial world, staying on course can be hard, especially when the curveballs come and you feel like you're in the middle of a storm. But no matter how chaotic things get, your North Star – your mission – is what keeps you grounded. It's the clear guide that directs your path, making sure you're always moving toward your bigger vision.

My mission? I help female entrepreneurs turn bold visions into tangible results. Lorraine's vision? Empowering women to achieve financial independence through property investment. Rich's mission? Changing the world, one powerful conversation at a time. Cody's mission? Helping online entrepreneurs create laid-back businesses that suit their lifestyles.

See how clear and easy these are to remember? That's the magic of nailing down your North Star. When your mission is distilled into a simple, repeatable statement, it not only sharpens your focus but also turns others into advocates who spread your word. Your mission becomes a beacon that people recognize and rally around, amplifying your impact.

Follow Your North Star

But having a North Star isn't just about having a catchy tagline; it's about discipline. It's about knowing exactly where you're headed and making sure every step you take gets you closer to that destination. In a world full of distractions and shiny objects, staying true to your mission means saying no – a lot.

Chasing rabbits

Let's get real about those distractions – those enticing opportunities that pop up, offering a quick win or a fun detour. I call these "chasing rabbits." They're tempting, and they might even seem like good ideas at the moment, but more often than not, they lead you off course.

Chasing rabbits is about getting sidetracked by things that don't really serve your bigger vision. They might look great on the surface, but they can pull you away from your true goals, draining your time, energy, and focus. The problem with these distractions is that they often masquerade as good opportunities when, in reality, they dilute your impact.

Before you leap into the next shiny opportunity, pause. Ask yourself, "Am I chasing rabbits here?"; If it's not aligned with your North Star, it's probably a distraction that will cost you more than it's worth.

Say 'No' to everything that doesn't align

Your time is your most valuable resource and there are already a lot of demands on it. Every 'yes' is a 'no' to something else. To stay aligned with your North Star, you need to get comfortable turning down anything that doesn't serve your mission. Every yes should be a deliberate choice that supports your mission. If it doesn't, that 'yes' could pull you off track.

Creating filters is key to this. These filters help you quickly assess whether an opportunity is worth your time and energy. Here are some of my most effective filters to keep you on track. Feel free to steal what's useful or create your own.

Alignment with vision

Does this opportunity clearly align with my long-term goals and mission? If it doesn't sync with my core values or vision, it's a definite no. Staying true to your North Star means being rock-solid in your commitment to what matters most.

Simplicity

Does this add unnecessary complexity? Simplicity is key. If an opportunity complicates things, it's a no. Keep your path streamlined to maintain momentum.

Freedom

Does this tie me down to someone else's timeline or agenda? If it compromises my freedom, it's a no. Freedom lets you pursue your mission on your terms.

Impact on progress

Will this move me forward, or is it a detour? Focus on actions that push you ahead, not sideways.

Time commitment

How much time will this take from my core activities? Can I minimize the time spent without missing out? Time is your most valuable resource-protect it.

Energy drain

Will this energise me or drain my energy? Where you spend your energy matters. Choose opportunities that uplift and sustain your momentum.

Return on investment

What's the potential return-on-investment – whether in time, energy, or resources? If it's not worth the investment, it's a no. Make sure your efforts pay off in ways that matter.

Gut feeling

Trust your intuition – if something feels off, it probably is. Your gut is often your best guide when the path isn't clear.

By applying these filters, you can stay aligned with your North Star, ensuring that every decision you make is purposeful and strategic. Saying 'no' becomes easier when you realize each 'no' is actually a 'yes' to something more meaningful and more aligned with your goals.

Stay true to your north star

Your North Star isn't just a mission statement – it's your compass. It's what keeps you moving forward, even when distractions try to pull you off course. Every time a new opportunity or idea crosses your path, take a moment to stop and ask yourself:

"Will this bring me closer to my bigger vision, or am I chasing rabbits?"

This question helps you stay true to your path, making sure every action you take is in service of your ultimate mission. Because when you follow your North Star, you're not just moving – you're moving with purpose, power, and unstoppable momentum.

CHAPTER 11

LEAVE NOTHING TO CHANCE

How you show up in the world isn't just important-it's everything. In today's digital age, your potential clients are forming opinions about you before you even meet them. This happens when they Google your name, browse your social media profiles, or visit your website-often while you're asleep. It might sound overwhelming, but here's the good news: when you approach building and managing your personal brand step by step, it's entirely manageable. And here's the kicker-most people won't take the time to do this work, which means that if you do, you'll naturally stand out from the crowd. Don't let this overwhelm you, choose the things that feel like low hanging fruit for you and build as you go!

Your online presence matters

In today's world, your online presence is often the first impression you make. What will potential clients find when they Google you? Is it a cohesive, professional, and engaging representation of who you are and what you stand for? Your digital footprint should be working for you, even when you're not actively managing it. This includes everything from your website to your social media profiles. When these elements are aligned and polished, they create a powerful, seamless experience that draws people in.

Own your personal domain

One of the most impactful steps you can take in building your personal brand is to own your 'ownname.com' domain. Even if your business operates under a different name, having a personal website that represents who you are and what you stand for is invaluable. Think of it as your digital calling card. Leaders like Richard Branson and Oprah Winfrey are known just as much for their personal brands as they are for their businesses. Your personal domain should at the very least host a one-page website that clearly communicates your mission, your values, and who you are as a person. It's about taking control of your online identity and ensuring that when people search for you, they find exactly what you want them to see.

Audit your digital footprint

Start by Googling yourself – yes, really. What comes up? Is it aligned with the brand you're building? If not, it's time to make some changes. Regularly audit your social media profiles, your website, and any other digital touchpoints to ensure they're up-to-date and reflective of your current brand. Remember, your potential clients are doing their homework on you, so give them something impressive to find.

Make it easy for clients to know, like, and trust you

Your online presence should be more than just a pretty face; it should be a strategic tool for building relationships. Think about what potential clients need to see, hear, and feel to know, like, and trust you. This means curating content that not only showcases your expertise but also humanises you. Share your story, your values, and your journey. Use testimonials, case studies, and social proof to build credibility. The goal is to create a digital presence that does the heavy lifting of relationship-building, so by the time someone reaches out, they already feel like they know you.

Optimize your website for conversion

Your website is your digital home base – it needs to not only look good but also work hard for you. Make sure it's designed with your ideal client in mind. Is it easy to navigate? Are there clear calls-to-action that guide visitors toward taking the next step? Whether it's booking a consultation, signing up for a newsletter, or making a purchase, your website should make it easy for potential clients to move from browsing to action.

Elevate your personal brand through visual consistency

Consistency is key when it comes to building a memorable brand. Your visual identity – colours, fonts, imagery – should be consistent across all platforms. This creates a cohesive look that reinforces your brand every time someone encounters it. But it's more than just looking good; it's about making sure that every visual element reflects the essence of your brand and speaks directly to your ideal clients.

Update your headshots

Your headshots are a vital part of your personal brand, so make sure they're up-to-date and reflective of the current, powerful version of you. But don't overdo it – while it's important to have high-quality images, you only need a handful of them. I've seen people sign up for photography memberships where they get new images every month, but that's way more than you need. A few well-chosen, impactful photos will serve you better than an endless stream of new ones.

Refine your elevator pitch

Your elevator pitch is your chance to make a strong, memorable impression quickly. It should be short, sharp, and easy for others to understand and repeat. Practice it in your business groups, keep it up to date, and tweak it until it lands perfectly with your audience. Don't try to be too clever with this-clarity beats creativity here. If others can't grasp it or repeat it, it's time to refine it further.

Get editorial coverage and publish guest articles

To boost your authority and reach, aim to get editorial coverage or publish guest articles. When people Google you, they shouldn't just find your content on your platforms – they should see your expertise validated on other reputable sites as well. This not only enhances your credibility but also expands your reach to new audiences. Whether it's through industry blogs, online magazines, or guest appearances on podcasts, getting your voice out there is key to establishing your authority.

Leverage storytelling to deepen connections

Your brand voice is the personality behind your words, and when paired with powerful storytelling, it's unstoppable. Your story is what makes you relatable and memorable. Share the highs, the lows, the wins, and the lessons learned along the way. Authenticity is what will resonate with your audience, so don't worry about perfection – focus on being real. This is how you humanise your brand and create deeper, more meaningful connections with your audience.

Embodying your brand every day

Your brand isn't just something you show online-it's how you show up in every aspect of your life. This is where my other book, *Unleash Your Inner Goddess*, comes into play. (I'll pop a QR code for that book at the end of the chapter in case you want to check it out). It's all about stepping out of your bedroom every morning ready to take on the world, embodying your mission with every breath you take. It's about tapping into your most powerful, authentic self and letting that energy shine through in everything you do. When you fully embrace and embody your brand, you're not just telling people who you are – you're showing them, with every word, every action, and every choice you make.

The power of consistency

Consistency is your best friend when it comes to building a brand that sticks. When you curate your brand with intention, you set yourself up to show up on autopilot – always aligned, always on point. Whether it's your visual identity, brand voice, or how you engage with your audience, consistency creates trust and recognition. The more consistent you are, the more your brand becomes second nature – not just for you, but for those who encounter it.

Create an actionable plan for continuous improvement

This isn't about overhauling everything at once. It's about taking small, intentional steps that build over time. Start by choosing one aspect of your brand to focus on each month.

Whether it's refining your social media presence, updating your website, or crafting a killer elevator pitch, pick one thing and do it well. Then, keep revisiting and refining – implementing small, 1% improvements each time.

The compound effect

Remember, these small, consistent efforts add up over time. As you keep making incremental improvements, you'll see how they compound to create a powerful, cohesive personal brand that truly leaves nothing to chance. By consistently showing up as the best version of yourself, you build a brand that's not only authentic and impactful but also unmistakably you.

To make this a fun and ever-evolving process, ask yourself this question weekly:

"What small step can I take to elevate my personal brand presence?"

Scan the QR code to go to the 'Unleash Your Inner Goddess' book

#2 UNLEASH YOUR INNER GODDESS

BECOME
UNSTOPPABLE

PART 3

BECOME UNSTOPPABLE

We would all love to keep all the balls in the air, all the time. But let's keep it real. Women essentially run the world, right? We're the ones who keep everyone's lives running smoothly, often putting ourselves last on the list. Is it any wonder we sometimes feel like we're stumbling through the day, only to wonder why we're not further along in our businesses?

We are fricking amazing – let's just own that right now. But being amazing doesn't mean we have to do it all the hard way. We want to remove as much friction as possible, clearing the path so we can soar. And here's the truth: for many of my clients, the biggest challenge isn't the competition or the market-it's getting out of their own way. Sound familiar?

I'd love to wave a magic wand and remove every obstacle in your path, but here's the deal – I need your help to make that happen. In Part 3, we're going to dive deep into what's really holding you back and uncover the ways to become truly unstoppable. We'll explore the habits, mindsets, and strategies that can help you step into your power and own just how badass you are.

You already have everything it takes-you just need to unleash it. So, let's get stuck in and start clearing the path to your unstoppable self!

CHAPTER 12

GET OUT OF YOUR OWN WAY

When I ask my clients what their biggest challenge is, the most frequent answer I hear is, "I get in my own way." This isn't just a passing comment, it's a universal challenge that even the most ambitious women face. We're often juggling multiple responsibilities: raising families, managing relationships, running households and businesses-and it's easy to feel like we're constantly falling short, getting stuck in our heads, overthinking every move.

The truth is, we can be our own worst enemy. And what I've noticed in conversations with women, is that we feel like we have to be 100% ready before we take action. We think everything has to be perfectly lined up, every detail sorted, every contingency planned. Meanwhile, men often feel ready to go when they're about 60% there. This need for perfection can be a massive roadblock, keeping us from taking the leaps we're more than capable of making.

Before we go any further, let's ground ourselves in self-compassion and grace. Recognise everything you've achieved so far, and celebrate it. You've already accomplished so much, and that's worth acknowledging. Now, let's dive into the top

13 ways we get in our own way and start removing these barriers, one by one.

The top 13 ways we get in our own way

Through countless conversations with my clients, these are the top 13 ways women tend to sabotage their own progress. Before we dive into how to overcome these challenges, take a moment to simply recognise which of these resonate with you. Awareness is the first step toward change, and understanding how these behaviours show up in your life is crucial.

"I don't have time"

Time often feels like it's slipping through your fingers, especially when you're juggling multiple roles and responsibilities. It's easy to feel overwhelmed and think there's never enough time to accomplish everything. The key is prioritising what truly matters and carving out time for those high-impact activities.

"I want to go in a new direction but don't know where to start"

The desire to pivot is both exciting and daunting. It's natural to feel unsure of where to begin when considering a new path. Rather than getting stuck in indecision, focus on taking the first small, deliberate step. Progress starts with action, no matter how small.

"Other people's beliefs about who I am and what I do are holding me back"

The expectations and opinions of others can create significant barriers, often making it difficult to pursue what you truly want. It's important to recognise that these external pressures don't define you. Breaking free from these constraints is essential for moving forward on your terms.

"I feel like an imposter"

Imposter syndrome can be a significant hurdle, especially when stepping outside your comfort zone. It's important to remember that these feelings are a natural part of growth. Every time you level up, you'll likely experience self-doubt, but that's a sign you're challenging yourself and expanding your capabilities.

"There are lots of ways I can help people, which one do I choose?"

Being multi-talented can lead to a sense of being pulled in too many directions. While it's a strength to have diverse skills, focusing on one area at a time can help you make a more meaningful impact. You can always explore other opportunities once you've gained traction in your chosen path.

"I'm afraid to niche"

Niching down can feel like a risk, as it may seem like you're narrowing your opportunities. However, specialising in one area can actually enhance your authority and make you stand out in a crowded market. Embracing a niche allows you to serve your audience more effectively.

"There's too much competition/somebody else is already doing that"

Competition can be daunting, but it's important to recognise that no one else has your unique perspective and approach. Your distinct voice and expertise are what set you apart. Rather than focusing on the competition, concentrate on what makes you uniquely qualified.

"Fear of failure paralyzes me"

The fear of failure can be a major obstacle, keeping you from taking necessary risks. It's important to shift your mindset and view failure as a learning experience rather than a setback. Each attempt brings you closer to success, even if it involves some missteps along the way.

"I'm waiting for the perfect moment"

Waiting for everything to be perfect before you start can lead to endless delays. The reality is that the perfect moment rarely arrives. The most successful people take action even when conditions aren't ideal, knowing that progress is better than perfection.

"I seek approval from others before taking action"

Seeking validation from others can slow down your decision-making and diminish your confidence. Trusting your own judgment and intuition is crucial. While feedback can be valuable, it's important not to rely solely on others' opinions to move forward.

"I'm afraid of standing out and being judged"

The fear of judgment can prevent you from fully expressing yourself and pursuing what you're passionate about. It's important to recognise that standing out is a necessary part of making an impact. Not everyone will agree with your choices, and that's okay.

"I don't feel ready or prepared enough"

It's common to feel like you need to be fully prepared before taking action, but waiting until you feel 100% ready can result in missed opportunities. Embrace the idea that growth often requires stepping into the unknown, even if you don't have all the answers.

"I compare myself to others"

Comparison can undermine your confidence and distract you from your own progress. It's important to focus on your unique journey and measure your success based on your own goals and achievements, rather than comparing yourself to others.

Shifting your internal narratives

Awareness is the first step to breaking free from these limiting beliefs. Once you recognise the stories you're telling yourself, you can begin to change them. Here's how:

Identify the limiting belief

Reflect on where you feel stuck and ask yourself, "What am I believing about myself in this situation?" Write it down, and then reframe it into a statement that empowers you. This is where transformation begins.

Take immediate action

Even the smallest step can ignite momentum. Action breaks the cycle of overthinking and creates a powerful feedback loop between your beliefs and behaviour, helping to lock in those new, empowering narratives.

Reflect and adjust

Regular reflection keeps you on track. Assess your progress, identify what's working, and make tweaks as needed. This continuous refinement ensures you stay aligned with your evolving goals and beliefs.

Develop a growth mindset

See challenges not as roadblocks but as stepping stones. Every obstacle is an opportunity to build resilience, sharpen your skills, and elevate your game.

Practice self-compassion

Be gentle with yourself when things don't go as planned. Self-compassion isn't about making excuses – it's about maintaining a constructive mindset that keeps you moving forward, even when you stumble.

Create a support system

Surround yourself with people who uplift and motivate you. A strong support network isn't just about accountability, it's about having a circle that fuels your drive and celebrates your wins.

Visualize success

Spend dedicated time visualising what success looks like for you. Picture the steps you'll take to get there. This practice isn't just daydreaming – it's about making your goals feel tangible and within reach.

Standing at the crossroads

Let's talk about those pivotal moments – the crossroads. Every time you level up, you'll find yourself standing at a fork in the road, facing choices that aren't always easy. These moments can be challenging, filled with uncertainty and the weight of deciding which path to take. I've been there many times, and through countless conversations with others, I've realised it's a place none of us enjoy. It often feels like time is slipping away as we wrestle with decisions, unsure of how to move forward.

In my own journey, especially in the fashion industry, I've navigated numerous pivots – from retail to wholesale, concessions, working with distributors, doing pop-ups, returning to retail, and eventually shifting to e-commerce. Each pivot was a crossroads, a moment where I had to decide which direction would lead me closer to my vision. And stepping into my next chapter as a coach and strategic partner to ambitious female entrepreneurs brought a whole new set of decisions.

At these crossroads, clarity and confidence are your greatest allies. The quicker you can cut through the noise and make those tough decisions, the sooner you can move forward to the part that truly matters – bringing your vision to life and making things happen. The key is not to get stuck at the crossroads but to use these moments as opportunities to realign with your purpose and move forward with intention.

Embrace your power

Remember, you have the power to change the story you tell yourself. By shifting your internal narratives and taking consistent action, you can transform self-doubt into self-belief and fear into confidence. Every small step you take is a victory over the limiting beliefs that have held you back.

Whenever you find yourself standing at the crossroads or feeling like you're getting in your own way, ask yourself:

"What's one tiny step I can take today to feel like I am moving forward?"

CHAPTER 13

THE POWER OF MINDSET SHIFTS

The story you tell yourself is the one that defines you-so make it a story of resilience, growth, and unstoppable success.

Start by recognising your own worth. You've got something unique to offer the world, and that's not by accident. You've built a strong foundation through your experiences and strengths, so stand firm in that. This is about knowing your value and letting it guide you forward.

The words you use about yourself matter. Your mind takes them to heart, so be kind and intentional with your self-talk. We're often our own toughest critics, zeroing in on where we think we've fallen short. But it's time to let that go. Instead, rewrite your story with compassion and strength. Focus on what you've learned and how far you've come.

When you catch yourself overthinking or getting in your own way, remember: you've done the work, and you're ready for what's next. This isn't about proving anything to anyone – it's about embracing who you are and where you're headed. Keep your narrative rooted in trusting yourself and let that be the foundation for your growth.

Let go of ruminating

Ruminating on past events can be a mental trap. We get caught up in worrying about what others think of us, replaying conversations and actions in our minds. But here's the reality: most people aren't thinking about us nearly as much as we imagine – they're too busy dealing with their own lives. Free yourself from this unnecessary burden by recognising that holding onto these thoughts doesn't serve you. Instead, ask yourself, "What can I learn from this?" and then let it go.

Reframe your stories

You have the power to change the narrative of any story you hold onto. While some experiences are undeniably painful and unjust, many of the meanings we attach to events can be transformed by revisiting them with a new perspective. Shift your mindset from "This happened *to* me" to "This happened *for* me." Look for the lessons, growth, and strength that came from those experiences. This shift in perspective turns challenges into opportunities and setbacks into stepping stones.

Embrace a growth mindset

A growth mindset isn't just some trendy concept-it's a game changer. When you believe that your abilities and intelligence can be developed through effort, learning, and persistence, you open yourself up to endless possibilities. Compare this to a fixed mindset, where you believe your capabilities are static and unchangeable, and it's clear why embracing growth is the way forward. It's about being resilient, adaptable, and ready to take on whatever comes your way, knowing that you can always learn and improve.

Daily affirmations

Incorporate daily affirmations into your routine. These aren't just feel-good statements – they're tools that can rewire your brain to think more constructively, pushing out self-sabotage and negativity. Use affirmations to build your self-belief and remind yourself of what you're capable of. Say them like you mean them: example:

"I am the architect of my own success, defining my path with vision, courage, and ease."

"I magnetise high-calibre opportunities and connections that expand my impact effortlessly."

"I lead boldly, with my own rules, creating a legacy that speaks long after I do."

"I navigate every season with grace, knowing that every shift strengthens my impact and purpose."

"I make decisions from a place of abundance, knowing I am always positioned for success."

"Every step I take aligns me deeper with my purpose and amplifies my reach."

Visualisation techniques

Visualisation is a powerful tool used by top performers across all fields. It's not just about daydreaming – it's about creating a vivid mental picture of your goals as if they've already been achieved. Spend a few minutes each day visualising your success. See it, feel it, hear it – make it real in your mind. This isn't just wishful thinking; it's mental rehearsal, prepping your brain for real-life action and boosting your confidence to make those dreams a reality.

Practice gratitude

Gratitude isn't just a buzzword – it's a mindset shift that can change your entire outlook. When you focus on what you're grateful for, you stop dwelling on what's missing and start appreciating what's already here. Start a daily gratitude journal where you jot down three things you're grateful for each day. It's a simple practice, but it can dramatically shift your mood, your mindset, and your overall sense of happiness.

Surround yourself with positivity

The people you surround yourself with can either lift you up or drag you down. So, choose your circle wisely. Spend time with those who inspire you, support you, and challenge you to be your best self. And don't be afraid to distance yourself from the energy vampires – those people who drain your energy or bring negativity into your life. Remember, you're in control of your environment, so curate it in a way that supports your growth.

Commit to continuous learning

A commitment to continuous learning is one of the most powerful things you can do for yourself. It keeps your mind sharp, your skills fresh, and your curiosity alive. Make it a habit to seek out new knowledge and experiences. Read books that stretch your thinking, take courses that enhance your skills, attend seminars that light a fire under you, and engage with communities that foster growth. This isn't just about staying relevant-it's about continuously evolving into the next best version of yourself.

By implementing these mindset shifts, you can transform your thinking and, ultimately, your life.

Whenever you're feeling less than inspired, ask yourself:

"What's one thought I can reframe today to see a challenge as an opportunity?"

CHAPTER 14

QUICK WINS FOR IMMEDIATE IMPACT

When my kids were growing up, the question I was asked most often was, "How do you do it all?" As the sole earner raising three kids on my own while building a business, I knew that if I wanted things to happen, it was on me to make them happen. There was nobody else to share the load, and let me tell you, that's a powerful motivator to dive in and make things happen. Over the years, I've learned to squeeze every drop of productivity out of my day. One of my go-to strategies? Setting a timer.

Seriously, it's like magic. You wouldn't believe how much you can accomplish when you put yourself on the clock, even if it's just for 15 or 20 minutes. I'm often amazed by what I can knock out and still have time left over to breathe. No matter how short on time you are, there's always room for quick wins, and, I'm always on the lookout for them.

Achieving quick wins is all about leveraging those small pockets of time and acting on your insights immediately. It's about making the most out of every moment and understanding that even the smallest actions can lead to significant progress.

Here are some strategies that have worked for me that might help you too.

Act on insights immediately

When you get an aha moment or insight, act on it right away, even if it's just taking the first tiny step or putting it in your diary. I've seen people have amazing breakthroughs in coaching sessions and then slide backward because they didn't take action. Insights are like sparks – if you don't fan the flame, it fades. So, the moment you get that spark, do something with it. Maybe it's jotting down a quick note, setting a reminder, or scheduling time to work on it. The key is to turn that initial spark into tangible progress, no matter how small. Consistent small actions add up to big results over time, and they prevent the overwhelm that comes from trying to tackle everything at once.

Action over analysis paralysis

We've all been there-stuck in analysis paralysis, overthinking every detail and delaying action. The key to breaking free from this trap is to prioritise action. When you have an idea or a moment of clarity, don't let it sit and gather dust. Take that first small, actionable step. The power of action lies in its ability to turn ideas into reality and create momentum. Remember, perfection is the enemy of progress. By focusing on taking action, even imperfectly, you can avoid getting bogged down in endless planning and start making meaningful progress toward your goals.

Test in the market

Instead of overthinking and planning every detail, put your idea out there. Gather real-world feedback and use it to refine and improve. The market is the ultimate test ground for your ideas. By launching quickly and iterating based on actual responses, you can avoid the paralysis of perfectionism and make meaningful progress. This approach not only saves time but also helps you create offerings that truly resonate with your audience.

Small steps matter

Don't get overwhelmed by the big picture. Break it down into manageable steps and tackle them one at a time. Each small step is progress. Achieving big goals often requires taking many small steps. By focusing on one task at a time, you maintain momentum and avoid feeling overwhelmed. Celebrate each small victory, as they collectively lead to significant achievements. Remember, consistent progress, no matter how small, adds up over time.

Pivot when needed

Be prepared to change direction based on feedback and results. Flexibility is key to adapting and growing. The ability to pivot is crucial in today's fast-paced environment. If something isn't working, don't be afraid to adjust your strategy. Stay open to new information and be willing to make changes. This adaptability allows you to stay relevant and responsive, ensuring your efforts are always aligned with your goals and market needs.

Leverage your network

Reach out to one person in your network every day. It could be for advice, feedback, or just to strengthen the relationship. Building and nurturing your network can lead to unexpected opportunities and support. These connections are invaluable, and investing a little time each day to maintain them can yield significant returns in terms of collaboration, ideas, and encouragement.

Declutter your workspace

Spend 10 minutes each day decluttering your workspace. A clean and organized environment can boost productivity and reduce stress, allowing you to focus better on your tasks. By creating a space that fosters clarity and concentration, you set yourself up for more effective work sessions and a clearer mind.

Set daily intentions

At the start of each day, set a clear intention for what you want to achieve. This helps you stay focused and motivated, ensuring that you make the most of your time. A simple practice of identifying your top three priorities can guide your actions throughout the day and keep you aligned with your goals.

Learn something new

Dedicate a small portion of your day to learning something new, whether it's reading an article, watching a tutorial, or listening to a podcast. Continuous learning keeps you sharp and opens up new possibilities. This habit not only enriches your knowledge but also sparks creativity and innovation in your work.

Celebrate small wins

Take a moment to celebrate your small wins each day. Recognising your progress, no matter how minor, can boost your morale and keep you motivated. Celebrating these victories reinforces positive habits and keeps your momentum going, making it easier to tackle bigger challenges.

The power of brainstorming

Never underestimate the power of brainstorming. This is the power of a thinking partnership. A quick back-and-forth conversation can move things along in minutes, cutting through the fog that might otherwise take days or even weeks of going around in circles. Whether it's a brainstorming session with a coach, mentor, or even a trusted colleague, these rapid exchanges can spark ideas, clarify your thinking, and set you on a faster path to achieving your goals.

Creating momentum even if you are time poor

Small steps build momentum. Instead of getting stuck in your head, create the habit of using tiny pockets of time to score quick wins. It might be 5 minutes while the kettle is boiling or while waiting for a meeting to start. Set a timer for 5 minutes and see what you can get done. It's amazing how much you can accomplish in those small bursts, and it's a great way to check off those little tasks that tend to pile up. This practice not only clears your to-do list but also gives you that satisfying feeling of kicking ass. So, ask yourself:

"What is a quick win I can get in the next 5 minutes?"

Try this every day for 30 days, and your life will change! Bring on those dopamine hits!

CHAPTER 15

SELF CARE: YOUR FIRST PRIORITY

Self-care isn't just about taking a break – it's about creating the time and space you need to think, recharge, and allow your bigger vision to flourish. It's also about supporting your physical well-being to sustain the drive and passion you bring to your work and your life. Sometimes, you have to be intentional about drawing the line, knowing when to stop for the greater good and your own longevity. This isn't always easy, especially when you're fuelled by ambition, but it's essential if you want to maintain your energy and focus over the long haul.

One of my absolute favourite ways to practice self-care is by taking a solo road trip. There's something magical about being in motion yet enveloped in silence. It's during these drives that I find clarity, creativity, and a deep sense of mental well-being. The combination of movement and quiet allows my mind to wander freely, often leading to breakthroughs and a renewed sense of calm.

What's your version of the solo road trip? Everyone has their own way of recharging, and it's crucial to discover what works best for you. Whether it's a quiet walk, a long bath, or simply sitting in silence, find what brings you peace.

In my own journey, I've learned that the time I take away from my business – whether it's crashing on the couch, hiking up a mountain with my daughter, or taking a long drive to clear my head-always pays off tenfold. It's about knowing when to push and when to pause.

Everyone has their own version of self-care and different energy levels, so it's crucial to pay attention to what works best for you. My coach, Rich Litvin, introduced me to a tool called an energy audit that I believe everyone should use. It's simple and highly effective:

- Write a list of things that give you energy.
- Write a list of things that drain your energy.
- Each month, remove one thing that drains your energy and add one thing that gives you energy. (If you can give it more time, ramp this up and do it every week!)

This simple practice can transform your life. Being intentional about your self-care isn't a luxury; it's a necessity. When you take care of yourself, you show up better in every aspect of your life. So, make self-care your priority and watch how it positively impacts your business and personal life.

Get into the habit of asking yourself:

Does this give me energy or drain my energy?

CHAPTER 16

UNSHAKEABLE CONFIDENCE: YOUR SECRET WEAPON

When my stores closed in March 2020 due to COVID, I thought this was it. This was the cliff there was no pivoting from. We were going over the edge, and there was nothing I could do about it. I was resigned to our fate. This was going to be the most epic failure of my 30 years in business.

It was March 2020, the start of a new season, and our new stock had landed earlier that week. I had two stores full of stock, enough to keep us going for six months, and we were in lockdown. Nobody was going anywhere. Those who couldn't work were hanging out on the couch in their PJs…those who were working were showing up on Zoom-presentable on their top half but wearing pjs on the bottom. The last thing anybody needed was designer clothes.

My daughter and I sat looking at each other. "What are we going to do?" she asked me. "What can we do? We'll figure it out…." I replied. The only thing I knew was that we had a window to enjoy our time together. She was between her undergrad and her master's, and we were taking a year to work together. So, we decided to lean into that and make the best of it. We started showing up online, sharing our behind-the-scenes antics. People became addicted; they told us afterward that they lived for our daily updates. It brought joy to their otherwise monotonous lockdown lives.

And then the weirdest thing happened: a steady stream of online orders started to come in, even while we slept. (We were lucky; while others in the fashion industry were scrambling to get online, we already had an e-commerce store.) By the end of 2020, we had not just cleared business loans and paid off investors, we had also sold every stitch of stock and built a pot of 12 months' running costs that gave me the head space I needed to figure out our next moves.

The biggest lesson in all this was to trust that somehow, everything will be okay. Just keep taking steps forward, trusting that each one will reveal the next. Trust yourself, and you'll navigate through the storms. There's always a way forward. Just remember who you are, harvest confidence from every win and learn from every failure as you go.

New level, new devil

Anytime we step into new levels, there will be moments that slow us down. It's natural to experience those wobbles when you're stepping into the unknown. But these challenges are often the very things that lead to our biggest opportunities. When the wobbles hit, remind yourself of your strengths, your superpowers, and the history you have of figuring things out. You've done it before, and you'll do it again.

Remember your power

You are more powerful than you realise. Think about

the times you've faced seemingly insurmountable challenges and come out stronger. You have a unique set of skills, experiences, and perspectives that no one else has. Your power lies in your perseverance and your ability to turn obstacles into opportunities. When doubt creeps in, remember that you've navigated stormy waters before – and this challenge is no different.

Introducing the ROCK framework

When life throws challenges your way and you start to feel off balance, my ROCK Framework is here to help you stay grounded. This framework is your go-to for regaining your footing and moving forward with confidence and clarity. Whether you're facing a minor wobble or a major storm, the ROCK Framework offers practical steps to help you stay aligned with your purpose and on track toward your goals.

The ROCK elements are:

R

RESILIENCE

For when you are feeling:

overwhelm | defeat | questioning your ability

Resilience is your ability to bounce back, no matter how hard you're hit. It's the inner strength that keeps you moving forward when everything around you feels like it's falling apart. When you're feeling overwhelmed, defeated, or questioning your ability to handle the challenges in front of you, resilience is what you need to tap into.

Ask yourself, "Am I staying strong in the face of challenges?"

Acknowledge the difficulties, but don't let them define you. You've weathered storms before and come out stronger-this time is no different. Stand tall and remember, resilience isn't about never falling; it's about rising every time you do.

Take some space and time to assess the situation objectively.

When emotions run high, perspective can get lost. Step back, take a deep breath, and evaluate the situation from a distance. What's the real challenge here? What's within your control, and what's beyond it? Clear thinking leads to clear solutions.

Remind yourself of your strengths and past obstacles you've overcome.

You've conquered challenges before – let those victories remind you of your power. Reflect on moments when you thought you couldn't, but you did. Let those memories be the fuel for your resilience today.

Identify any negative self-talk and reframe it positively.

The voice in your head can either uplift or undermine you. Spot any negative self-talk and challenge it. Reframe those thoughts into powerful affirmations that remind you of your strength and capability.

Practice self-care: Are you sleeping well, eating healthily, and taking breaks?

Resilience isn't just mental; it's physical too. Your body needs to be in top shape to support your mind. Prioritise sleep, nutrition, and regular breaks to recharge and keep your resilience strong.

Set boundaries to protect your mental and emotional well-being.

Know your limits and protect your energy fiercely. It's okay to say no to things that drain you, and yes to the things that nurture your spirit. Your resilience thrives when you guard your peace.

O

OWNERSHIP

For when you are feeling:

out of control | distracted | tempted to shift blame

Ownership is about taking full responsibility for your actions, your results, and your life. It's about stepping up and owning both your successes and your failures without blaming others or external circumstances. When you feel out of control, easily distracted, or tempted to shift blame, it's time to focus on ownership.

Ask yourself, "Where am I out of alignment?"

Take a hard, honest look at your actions. Do they match your values and goals? Identify where you've veered off course and what needs to change to bring you back in line with your true path.

Are you staying focused or getting distracted by shiny objects?

Shiny objects can be tempting, but they often lead you astray. Stay laser-focused on your goals, and resist the pull of distractions. Remember, every time you say yes to something new, you might be saying no to what really matters.

What are you doing that you need to stop?

Progress often means letting go. Identify habits or activities that are no longer serving you and have the courage to cut them out. Make room for what truly moves the needle.

What are you avoiding?

Avoidance is often a form of self-sabotage. Face what you've been dodging head-on and take steps to deal with it. Growth happens when you tackle what's uncomfortable.

Are you playing to your strengths?

When you operate in your zone of genius, everything flows. Lean into what you do best and let go of the rest. Playing to your strengths isn't just effective – it's energising.

Take action steps towards your goals, even if they are small.

Every step forward counts, no matter how small. Momentum builds with each action, so keep moving, even if it's just an inch at a time.

Avoid blaming others or external circumstances.

Ownership means taking full responsibility. Blaming others or circumstances gives away your power – owning your journey takes it back. You're in control of your path, and that's where your power lies.

Revisit your values and goals to ensure your actions align with them.

Regular check-ins with your core values and goals keep you aligned and focused. Make sure your daily actions reflect what truly matters to you, so you stay on course.

C

CLARITY

For when you are feeling:

confused | aimless | uncertain

Clarity is about cutting through the noise and confusion to see your path clearly. It's about understanding your goals, your direction, and the steps you need to take. If you're feeling confused, aimless, or uncertain, focusing on clarity will help you find your way.

Ask yourself, "Do I need to regroup or realign?"

Sometimes, the path gets blurry, and that's okay. Step back, reassess, and if necessary, adjust your course. Regrouping isn't a setback; it's a powerful way to ensure you're still headed in the right direction.

Revisit your mission statement and ensure it still resonates with you.

Your mission statement is your guiding star. If it no longer reflects your journey, it's time to refine it. Make sure it's something that excites and motivates you every day.

Simplify your goals and focus on what truly matters.

Complexity can create confusion. Strip away the non-essentials and focus on the goals that have the biggest impact. Ask yourself, "What would this look like if it were easy?" and then make it just that.

Clear out distractions and focus on your core priorities.

Distractions dilute your focus and energy. Clear them out, and direct your attention to your core priorities. This is where your true power lies.

Ask for feedback to ensure you are having the intended impact.

Sometimes we need an outside perspective to see clearly. Seek feedback from trusted mentors or colleagues to ensure you're on track and making the impact you intend.

Visualise your end goals to maintain focus and direction.

Keep the big picture front and centre. Visualising your end goals helps you stay focused, motivated, and on course, even when the road gets tough.

K

KINDLING

For when you are feeling:

unmotivated | burnt out | disconnected

Kindling is about keeping your inner fire alive-your passion, motivation, and drive. It's what fuels you to keep going, even when the journey gets tough. If you're feeling unmotivated, burnt out, or disconnected, it's time to rekindle that fire.

Ask yourself, "Am I fuelling my passion and staying motivated?"

Passion is your power source. Are you nurturing it? Reignite your passion by focusing on what excites you most, and watch your motivation soar.

Are you operating in your zone of genius? If not, delegate.

Your energy spikes when you're working in your zone of genius. If you're bogged down by tasks that drain you, it's time to delegate. Focus on what you do best and let others handle the rest.

Are you focusing on the most impactful tasks, or are you busy being busy?

Don't confuse activity with progress. Identify the tasks that truly make a difference and prioritise them. Being busy isn't the goal – being effective is.

Set short-term goals that give you a sense of accomplishment.

Small wins build big momentum. Set short-term goals that are achievable and celebrate each one. These victories keep your fire burning and push you forward.

Surround yourself with inspiring and supportive people.

Energy is contagious. Surround yourself with people who lift you up, challenge you, and inspire you to be your best. They're the spark that keeps your fire lit.

Learn something new that can contribute to your growth.

Growth fuels motivation. Dive into a new skill, explore a new interest, or challenge yourself with something unfamiliar. Learning keeps your mind sharp and your spirit alive.

Take time to reflect on your achievements and celebrate them.

Don't rush past your successes. Acknowledge and celebrate what you've accomplished. It's the fuel that will keep your fire burning bright.

Whenever you feel the wobbles, ask yourself:

"What element of my ROCK needs reinforcing?"

Identify which part of the ROCK Framework – Resilience, Ownership, Clarity, or Kindling – needs your attention right now. Reflect on your current challenges and consider which element, if strengthened, could make the most significant impact on your confidence and progress. By focusing on the specific area that needs reinforcement, you can take targeted actions to regain your footing and propel yourself forward.

SUCCESS ON YOUR TERMS

PART 4

SUCCESS ON YOUR TERMS

Success isn't one-size-fits-all – it's a journey that evolves as you do. The world might glorify seven-figure+ businesses and sky-high revenue, but true success runs deeper than numbers. It's about creating a life that's fiercely aligned with your values, your wildest dreams, and the impact you're here to make.

In this part of the book, we're breaking free from conventional definitions of success and building something that's uniquely yours. This isn't about keeping up with the hustle or chasing someone else's version of achievement. It's about asking yourself, "What does success really mean to me?" and then having the courage to create it, whether that means shooting for the stars or savouring the success you've already built.

We'll reverse-engineer your goals so every move you make is deliberate, powerful, and aligned with your true vision. We'll explore the power of innovation – because in a world that's constantly changing, the freedom to pivot and evolve is your greatest asset. And as your vision continues to expand, remember that success is as much about knowing when to reach higher as it is about knowing when to enjoy where you are.

This isn't just about hitting milestones – it's about defining what's possible on your terms and building a life that feels right for you. Whether you're aiming for the next big leap or relishing the fruits of your labour, this part is your roadmap to success that's deeply personal and endlessly fulfilling.

So, as you dive into these chapters, keep this question close:

"What does success look like on my terms, and how will I embrace and create it?"

CHAPTER 17

YOUR VERSION OF FINANCIAL SUCCESS

When my marriage ended, I found myself facing a daunting financial reality. The day I received a call from my bank manager, informing me that my mortgage was six months in arrears, was a wake-up call I hadn't anticipated. The shock quickly turned into resolve. I knew I had to take action-not just to survive, but to secure a stable future for my family. That was the moment I realised that financial freedom wasn't about hitting a specific number. It was about having enough to do what I wanted, to provide for my children, and to live a life that felt fulfilling and true to my values.

Redefining success: breaking free from society's standards

For many women, financial success is often defined by society's standards – revenue, profits, net worth. But those metrics don't always tell the full story. Financial success can mean different things to different people. For some, it's about earning enough to fund their lifestyle. For others, it's about having the freedom to take time off when they want or to pursue passion projects without financial strain. The challenge is to redefine what financial success means on your own terms and not get caught up in the rat race of others' definitions.

Aligning finances with what truly matters

The key to defining financial success is to start by understanding what truly matters to you. Reflect on your values, your goals, and your dreams. Ask yourself: What does success look like for me? Is it about security, freedom, impact, or perhaps a combination of these? Once you have clarity, you can align your financial goals with your personal values. This alignment allows you to pursue financial success without compromising on the things that matter most – whether that's your health, relationships, or time for personal growth.

Visualising your financial future

One practical approach is to create a financial vision board. This isn't just about numbers; it's about visualizing the life you want to lead. Include images and words that represent your financial goals and how they tie into your desired lifestyle. Keep this board in a place where you can see it daily – I like to use the home screen on my phone. It will serve as a constant reminder of what you're working toward and help you stay focused on your true financial priorities.

As you reflect on these ideas, it's essential to consider this:

What does financial success mean to you, and how can you align your financial goals with the life you truly want to live?

CHAPTER 18

REVERSE ENGINEER YOUR SUCCESS

In my 30 years of business, I've often found myself needing to reverse-engineer success. One of the most vivid examples is when I transitioned my fashion business from brick-and-mortar stores to online sales. It was a daunting task, especially when I had to do it overnight due to unforeseen circumstances. When COVID closed my stores, somehow, I didn't panic, even though 6 months' worth of stock had just landed for the season ahead, along with all of the fabric, production, and marketing invoices.

Over the years, I had developed the habit of reverse engineering everything – from buying my ex out of the house to sending my kids to private school. These were things that, as a single mother supporting three kids on her own financially, I probably shouldn't have been able to do. Sometimes I look back and wonder how on earth I kept all the balls in the air, but it was because I was reverse-engineering everything.

So as I sat in my office in the midst of the COVID shitshow, I knew I'd figure it out…I just needed to breath and take it one step at a time.

Somewhere along the journey of running my business, I fell in love with the numbers. I know so many entrepreneurs who cringe when I talk about numbers, but honestly, they always tell a story. If you keep track of them over time, they add a layer of depth to your insights that is pure gold. These days, I always project my cashflow out three years so I can see the impact of embracing or rejecting ideas and opportunities. What's worth my time, what's not – it's all there in the projections. Now, don't get me wrong, aside from my projections activities, I pretty much leave the accounting stuff to my accountant (yuck!). Once I know what I'm aiming for, I get to work. Once I'm hitting my milestones, I can step away from focusing on the numbers and give my energy over to the fun part of business-delivery.

Instead of panicking when faced with a challenge, I start with the end goal in mind. My focus isn't just to survive but to thrive, whether it's in the digital space or any other venture I take on. I plot my milestones, break down the steps required to achieve this new version of success and get to work.

The overwhelm of financial goal setting

When faced with a significant challenge or a lofty goal, it can be difficult to know where to start. This is where reverse engineering comes in. By working backward from your end goal, you can create a clear, step-by-step plan that feels manageable and actionable.

Start with the end in mind

Reverse engineering is all about beginning with your ultimate goal and then working backward to outline the steps needed to achieve it. Think of it as creating a detailed roadmap: you set your destination first, and then identify the key milestones that will guide you there. This approach brings clarity and confidence because it transforms a daunting goal into a series of manageable, actionable steps.

To truly harness the power of reverse engineering, start by asking yourself:

> *"What is my ultimate goal, and what are the key milestones I need to reach to achieve it?"*

But don't stop there – take it a step further. Once you've plotted out your milestones, think about the various activities that can generate the income you desire. Consider the time, effort, and resources each activity will require, and then forecast their potential impact over the next three years. This isn't just about reaching your income goals; it's about assessing which activities are truly worth your time and energy.

Sit with the numbers. Look at the work you'll have to do for different price points and offerings. Which activities align best with the financial freedom and time freedom you want for yourself? Which ones allow you to make the biggest impact in the world while also supporting the lifestyle you desire?

I have used this system for several years now and it is so powerful that I decided to develop an app to make it effortless for others to do the same. **ForecastApp** allows you to explore and compare the impact of potential activities on your finances over the next 3 years. It's a game-changer for gaining clarity on where to focus your efforts. You can check it out using the QR code at the end of this chapter.

By taking the time to carefully evaluate your options, you can make informed decisions about which paths will bring you the greatest returns – both financially and in terms of the impact you want to make. Remember, it's not just about working harder; it's about working smarter, ensuring that every step you take is aligned with your long-term vision.

With this approach, you're not just setting goals – you're strategically designing a future that excites you and propels you toward the success you've always envisioned.

Scan the QR code to find out more about the
FORECASTAPP

#3 FORECASTAPP

CHAPTER 19

INNOVATE YOUR WAY TO FREEDOM

Innovation has always been at the heart of my entrepreneurial journey. From creating new fashion lines each season to pivoting my business model during turbulent times, I've always believed in the power of staying ahead of the curve. When the pandemic hit and my physical stores had to close, I knew I couldn't just wait for things to return to normal. Instead, I took action. I quickly transitioned my business online, created new products, and found creative ways to engage with my customers. This approach didn't just save my business-it opened up new revenue streams that I hadn't even considered before. Innovation is my lifeline, it's a mindset I carry with me in everything I do.

Staying relevant in a rapidly changing world

In a world that's constantly evolving, standing still is not an option. Whether you're dealing with market disruptions, technological advancements, or shifting customer needs, the ability to innovate is crucial to staying relevant and forging ahead. I know the idea of innovation can be intimidating, especially if you're used to doing things a certain way. The fear of change can keep you stuck, but in today's landscape, standing still is the riskiest move you can make.

Embrace curiosity and experimentation

To innovate successfully, start by embracing a mindset of curiosity and experimentation. Be willing to question the status quo and explore new possibilities. Innovation doesn't always mean reinventing the wheel – it can be as simple as finding a more efficient way to do something or offering your customers a new experience. The key is to stay open to change and see challenges as opportunities for growth. Innovation isn't a one-time event; it's a continuous habit of learning, adapting, and evolving.

Fuelling innovation: the power of brainstorming and challenging your perspective

Incorporate regular brainstorming sessions into your routine. Get in a room with people who challenge your worldview. Hire a coach who isn't afraid to say the things others won't, someone who's there to serve, not please. Set aside time each week to think creatively about your business. Challenge your current view of everything and anything, big things and small things. Imagine what things would look like if you couldn't fail, or if you changed a limiting belief. Ask yourself questions like, "What's one thing I could do differently to elevate my customer experience?" or "What new revenue streams could I explore?" or "If I was starting this from scratch, what would I keep and what would I ditch?". Keep a journal of your ideas and revisit them regularly. Sometimes, the breakthrough you need is sitting in that notebook, waiting for the right moment.

Innovation is your path to freedom and financial security.

Ask yourself regularly:

> *"What bold, new idea can I experiment with today to push my business forward and create the future I desire?"*

This isn't just about business — it's about creating a future that aligns with your vision and values. The best time to innovate is now.

CHAPTER 20

EVOLVING YOUR VISION THE ART OF EXPANDING

As we evolve, so do our visions. For many of my clients, this shift happens after they've accomplished major milestones in life – they've raised their families, mastered their craft, and achieved significant success. They find themselves at a crossroads, craving something more – a deeper impact, a new challenge, a chance to expand beyond what they've already achieved. I've been there too. Designing collections that made my customers feel great was fulfilling for a long time, but eventually, it wasn't enough. I wanted to go deeper, to make a more profound impact.

That curiosity led me to coaching, where I found immense satisfaction in helping others unlock their potential. But even that wasn't the end. As that journey evolved, I realized that my true calling was to help women like me aim for their impossible dreams and soar higher than they ever thought possible. The more I walked into this vision, the bigger and bolder it became. This journey of continuous evolution is the essence of creating success on your own terms and breaking away from what everyone else is doing.

Facing the crossroads of success

Many entrepreneurs reach a point where their initial vision no longer excites or challenges them. They've achieved what they set out to do, but now they're left wondering, "What's next?" This stage can be both exhilarating and daunting. The challenge lies in allowing yourself to evolve, to dream bigger, and to pursue a new vision that may look entirely different from where you started. It's about embracing the unknown and being open to where the journey takes you.

Embrace the evolution

To evolve your vision, you must first give yourself permission to want more – more impact, more challenge, more fulfilment. Start by reflecting on what excites you now, what you're passionate about, and what kind of legacy you want to leave behind. Understand that your vision doesn't have to be static; it can grow and change as you do. Embrace the idea that your next chapter might be something you've never imagined before, and that's what makes it exciting. Stay open to new possibilities and trust that your journey will unfold as it should, even if it takes you in unexpected directions.

A final spark to ignite your next chapter

As you evolve into your next chapter or rise up to your next audacious level, remember that the evolution of your vision is not just about expanding your business or career; it's about expanding your possibility. The journey ahead is filled with unknowns, but that's where the magic happens. The path you take may twist and turn in ways you never anticipated, but each step is an opportunity to redefine what's possible for you.

The story doesn't end here — it's just beginning. What if the boldest version of your vision is yet to come? What if you're only scratching the surface of what you're truly capable of? As you step into this next chapter, keep asking yourself:

What's the next impossible dream I'm ready to make possible?

CHAPTER 21

THE MAGNETIC CODE

You've made it this far, so take a moment to celebrate the journey you've been on – even before you picked up this book. You've uncovered and harnessed the badass energy that's been with you all along, the drive that's pushed you to dig deep, face challenges, and rise above them. This isn't just about taking in more information-it's about taking those micro insights you've gathered and infusing them into your unique blend, creating a recipe that's undeniably hot.

You've already got the foundation, the grit, and the drive – now it's time to turn up the heat. As you move forward, remember that this isn't just about playing the game; it's about owning it. *The Magnetic Code* principles that follow are your guide to keeping that fire blazing, each one a touchstone to remind you of the powerhouse you are.

Embrace them, tweak them, make them yours. This is an ever-evolving journey of impact, fun, and success on your terms. Pick one, run with it, then come back for more when you're ready to level up again. This is your time to shine, and the only limits are the ones you set for yourself.

The Magnetic Code : 10 guiding principles

1. Unleash your secret sauce

Remember who you are – every twist and turn of your journey, every strength, every unique trait that sets you apart. Your secret sauce is your superpower. It's the rock you stand on, your home ground to return to whenever you need to regroup, boost your confidence, navigate a pivot, or rise to a new level. Keep building on your experience, stay grounded in your value, and never forget the immense power you bring to the world. This is your foundation – unshakable, unbreakable, and uniquely yours.

2. Define your north star

Your North Star is your guiding light, your evolving vision that keeps you moving forward. Don't just set it and forget it – let it grow with you. Look to the future regularly, and make sure your vision keeps getting braver, bolder, and spicier. Practice courage in the small things so it becomes second nature when it's time to take on the big challenges. The more you stretch your vision, the more you expand your potential. Get ready for your game to keep levelling up.

3. Embody confidence

Confidence isn't a one-size-fits-all concept; it's a habit that you cultivate in your own way. What makes you feel like the most badass version of yourself? Is it the clothes you wear, the workouts that make you feel invincible, or the thrill of a successful product launch? Find what works for you and make it a regular part of your routine. And remember, confidence boosters don't have to be grand gestures – sometimes, it's the little things that pack the biggest punch. A power pose, a few minutes of focused breathing, or a killer outfit can all elevate your confidence in a flash.

4. Balance passion with strategy

Passion fuels your fire, but strategy is the map that guides your journey. It's not enough to be passionate – you need a clear plan to channel that passion into actionable steps. Marry the two and you create a business that is not only inspired but also sustainable. Your passion gives you the drive, while your strategy gives you the direction. Together, they're unstoppable. Make sure your strategy aligns with your passion, and you'll find that your work not only excites you but also brings tangible results.

5. Operate in your zone of genius

Your zone of genius is where you're unstoppable. It's the sweet spot where your strengths, passions, and skills converge. Focus on what you do best, and delegate the rest. When you operate in your zone of genius, you're not just working – you're thriving. You're delivering your highest value to the world, and in return, you receive the greatest rewards. Don't dilute your genius by getting bogged down in tasks that drain you. Stay in your zone, and watch your impact soar.

6. Lead with purpose

Leading with purpose means being crystal clear on your vision and ensuring that everything you do aligns with it-including the people you choose to work with. Surround yourself with those who share your values and your mission. When your team is united in purpose, everyone rises together in a culture that enriches the lives of all involved. Make your purpose the driving force behind every decision, and you'll create a legacy that goes far beyond business.

7. Own your journey

The highs, the lows, and everything in between – own it all. Take responsibility not just for your successes but also for your mistakes, and the mistakes of your team. Be a force to be reckoned with and a safe harbour when things go sideways. When the shit hits the fan, don't point fingers – step up, take charge, and lead with strength and integrity. Your journey is yours to own, and by embracing it fully, you become the leader that others aspire will follow to the ends of the earth.

8. Adapt & pivot

The ability to adapt and pivot is one of your greatest strengths. Remember the power of the one-degree pivot — those tiny, almost imperceptible adjustments that can take you in a completely new direction over time. Whether it's a major shift or a subtle tweak, be ready to adjust your course when needed. Stay flexible, stay open, and trust that every pivot is taking you closer to your ultimate destination.

9. Innovate fearlessly

Innovation isn't just about the big ideas-it's about practicing courageous action in the small things. Don't shy away from hard conversations, honour your boundaries with kindness, and be a badass with grace. These small acts of courage build an internal foundation so solid that you'll step fearlessly into the unknown. Keep innovating, even in the tiniest ways – surprise your clients, draw inspiration from different industries, and never stop pushing the envelope. Your fearless innovation will set you apart and keep you ahead of the curve.

10. Prioritise self-care

Your most valuable asset is your health – protect it fiercely. Prioritize your energy and commit to your longevity so you can keep going on your terms. Self-care isn't a luxury; it's a necessity. It's what allows you to show up fully in your business and your life. Whether it's through regular exercise, meditation, or simply taking time to recharge, make self-care a non-negotiable part of your routine. You're in this for the long haul, so make sure you're taking care of the one person who matters most — you.

11. Bonus principle: success is always on your terms

Success isn't about fitting into someone else's mould- it's about defining it for yourself. Be clear on what success means to you across all areas of your life-financial, relational, personal, and professional – and pursue it unapologetically. Your version of success is the only one that matters, so don't let anyone else's expectations dictate your journey. Own your definition of success and go after it with everything you've got.

As we wrap things up, I want to take a moment to reflect on the journey we've been on together. I hope you've uncovered some golden threads – those connections between your past experiences, unique strengths, and your purpose and vision. My wish for you is that you never forget who you are and how powerful you truly are. Let go of second-guessing yourself, and step boldly into the world to shake things up, creating the impact and legacy that you desire.

Remember, when you're fully dialled into your own power, the competition doesn't even matter. You're in a league of your own, and your unique strengths will naturally shine through. Take what you've uncovered in this book and share it – lift others up with the insights you've gained, letting your journey be the spark that inspires those around you.

CHAPTER 22

NEXT STEPS

The truth is, you don't need a coach or a strategy partner – you've got everything within you to create the success you desire. But here's the thing: having someone in your corner to challenge your thinking, clear roadblocks, and help you go bigger can catapult you from good to extraordinary. I've invested heavily in coaching myself because I know that the right support accelerates your growth, pushes you past your limits, and helps you unlock the version of you that's truly unstoppable.

If you're ready to elevate your journey and step into your next level of success, visit marygrant.com. Let's see how we can make magic happen-together.

Visit marygrant.com here…

#4 MARYGRANT.COM

ACKNOWLEDGEMENTS

My 31 years as an entrepreneur have been a wild ride. Back when I started, there were no websites, no social media, no online business world. Business was local; reaching clients on the other side of the world meant getting on a plane. My business has gone through so many iterations over that time. On several occasions, I found myself at the edge of a cliff, pivoting just in time to avoid a spectacular crash. I have learned so much from the people I've come in contact with – my early-day mentors, my customers along the way, my bricks-and-mortar team. There are too many to mention everyone, but a few who may not even know the impact they had on my business and journey as a single mum trying to keep all the balls in the air include Bernie and Sean Flanagan, Brid Fallon, Marion Cuddy, Kate Gaffney, Louise Flanagan, Kate O'Dwyer, Jenny Turner, Dorothy Ronan, Nikki Creedon, Shelly Corkery, Stephen Sealey, and Barbara Burke.

When I discovered the online business world, my mind was blown. I immersed myself in learning from masters in their niche: Daniel Priestly, Rich Litvin, James Wedmore, Stu McLaren, Taki Moore, Cody Burch, Amy Porterfield, Susie Moore, Mel Abraham, Colin Boyd. I have invested (I won't say how much) in their programs and coaching. Along the way, my vision expanded into something bigger than I ever thought possible. I started to see how I could serve my future clients on a whole new level. My vision became clear: to create a ripple effect of empowered, unstoppable women who know their worth, own their story, and lead with unshakeable confidence. This book is just one piece of that vision – a vision where women everywhere rise beyond their limits, stepping boldly into spaces they once thought out of reach, leaving their unique mark on the world. That legacy is the ultimate win – the knowledge that my journey and the lessons within these pages might fuel another's rise to greatness, helping her see that she, too, can reach for more, redefine what's possible, and rewrite her story.

A special shoutout to Rich Litvin and Daniel Priestley. I participated in one of their deep dive coaching events, and when Daniel asked me what I wanted to get from our time together, I said, "I want to be catapulted over the wall." He asked me what I meant. I said "I have no idea but that's my vision!" We both laughed, but this whimsical moment now actually reminds me of what I want to do for others: catapult them to their next level of impact and success. Thank you, Daniel, for meeting me where I was at and challenging my thinking on what was possible. Thank you, Rich Litvin, for seeing and showing me how powerful I am and for challenging me to step up and honour my own journey and impossible goals.

BOOK RESOURCES

THE BRAND ARCHETYPE ASSESSMENT

#1 THE PERSONAL BRAND ARCHETYPE
ASSESSMENT

UNLEASH YOUR INNER GODDESS (BOOK)

#2 UNLEASH YOUR INNER GODDESS

FORECAST APP

#3 FORECASTAPP

NEXT STEPS

#4 MARYGRANT.COM

www.ingramcontent.com/pod-product-compliance
Ingram Content Group UK Ltd.
Pitfield, Milton Keynes, MK11 3LW, UK
UKHW020036050525
458189UK00001B/2